INTRODUCTION: MAOISM VS. BOLSHEVISM, LETTER TO A COMRADE IN THE UNITED KINGDOM

By Steve Clark

406 West Street
New York, NY 10014

June 6, 1998

Dear Comrade,

The request from some comrades in the United Kingdom to reprint *The Catastrophe in Indonesia*, as well as a similar request from some comrades here in New York, prompted a discussion in the Socialist Workers Party Political Committee on several political questions that we wanted to raise with you.

The pamphlet was published in 1966 by Merit Publishers, Pathfinder's predecessor. Pathfinder subsequently withdrew it from publication because of the political line of Ernest Mandel's article, which reflected his view that Maoism was left centrist in character rather than counterrevolutionary Stalinist. It was a political error for the *Militant* to have run an excerpt from Mandel's article in the "Book of the Week Column" in its April 6 issue. Ma'mud [Shirvani]'s comments in the April 20 issue—pointing out that "the article fails to draw the central lesson: the treacherous role of Stalinism in leading the masses to defeat without a battle"—should have been printed as a special feature correcting the error. Instead, it was relegated to the letters column, where readers had no reason to believe it reflected anything more than one person's opinion.

What is in some ways most notable about both the decision of the *Militant* editor to run the Mandel excerpt and the proposals to reprint the 1966 pamphlet is that comrades did not do the political work beforehand to go back and mine the rich record of the communist movement over many decades—the political continuity of the revolutionary working class, conquered in blood. Few did the hard but rewarding work to find out what our movement had written in the past about the struggles against Dutch imperialism and the revolutionary movement in Indonesia, the counterrevolutionary consequences of the Maoist variety of Stalinism, or even the 1965 massacre itself. This is similar to what we discussed in the international leadership a couple of years ago, when the comrades in the leadership of the SWP and other communist leagues responsible for the reporting teams to France during the wave of workers struggles in late 1995 and early 1996 did not prepare themselves and other comrades by studying the firsthand coverage and analysis of the May–June 1968 upsurge from the *Militant* and *Intercontinental Press* collected in the booklet *Revolt in France*.

This time around, the resources available are, if anything, even more plentiful. *World Outlook*—the meticulously mimeographed forerunner of *Intercontinental Press*, edited by Joseph Hansen—ran numerous news accounts and analyses of the 1965–66 events in Indonesia; many were reprinted in the pages of the *Militant*. In the 1940s and 1950s our magazine, now easily accessible through the *New International on CD-ROM*, carried numerous informative articles on the struggle for national liberation and socialism in Indonesia in this century, written by revolutionists in that country as well as in the Netherlands, the colonial power. The books, pamphlets, and Education for Socialists bulletins published and distributed by Pathfinder record the lessons of our class from the Chinese revolution and other post–World War II social overturns, the fight for workers and farmers governments, and the counterrevolutionary course of Stalinism from its origins to its accelerated disintegration over the past decade. Not to mention the internal bulletins of our world movement, several of the most pertinent of which I will refer to below.

When the pamphlet *The Catastrophe in Indonesia* was originally published in 1966, the Fourth International had just been reunified three years earlier. Central to the decade-long split had been the course by those in the current of which Mandel was a leader of adapting to Stalinist and centrist forces, instead of charting a steady communist course to build proletarian parties. Reunification had been achieved on the basis of a converging political response to the Cuban revolution and its communist leadership, as well as to the openings created by the initial, post–1956 manifestations of the disintegration of world Stalinism.

The October 1965 slaughter in Indonesia, in which hundreds of thousands of workers and Communist Party supporters were killed, was the most devastating defeat for the working class since the fascist victory in Germany in 1933. As Socialist Workers Party leader Joseph Hansen wrote in his introduction to the 1966 pamphlet, the defeat in Indonesia "had grave repercussions for the colonial revolution, the workers' states and the socialist struggle in general. . . . The most spectacular immediate result [of the defeat] is to be seen in China. The evidence strongly indicates that it was the precipitating cause for the 'Cultural Revolution,' which has so surprised and puzzled the Sinologists."[1]

In 1965–66, the SWP leadership and those who shared our views in the world movement anticipated that lessons drawn from these momentous events in Indonesia and in China itself could alter the thinking on Stalinism of some in the Fourth International majority, just as the defeat in Germany in 1933 had drawn a layer of revolutionary-minded workers and youth in and around the CP to communist conclusions. It was with that goal in mind that we agreed to collaborate in producing a pamphlet that contained the Mandel article, as well as an introduction by Hansen (a Marxist assessment of these events that retains its political value), a statement by the United Secretariat of the Fourth International, and an account of the disastrous course of the Indonesian CP by a young member of that party who had made his way into exile.

---

1. Hansen's introduction is reprinted in this Education for Socialists publication.

In hindsight, the impact and trajectory we had hoped for at the time did not come about. No qualitatively different articles on Maoism or Indonesia were written by Mandel or others in his current. But politics is not conducted in hindsight, and during the period the pamphlet was produced we were working with comrades around the world with the aim of advancing political clarity and homogeneity as a basis for common action in the class struggle. (For similar reasons, we also collaborated in 1968 to produce a collection of articles, with an introduction by Mandel, entitled *Fifty Years of World Revolution: 1917–1967.* Although this was made up of longer think pieces—a "colloquium," as George Novack liked to say—the impact of events between 1968 and 1975 did not yield a more communist colloquium, and Merit subsequently withdrew that book from publication.)

The resolutions adopted at the reunification congress in 1963 had seemed to mark a degree of political convergence on the assessment of the Chinese Communist Party, as had the draft of a resolution on the Sino-Soviet conflict that Hansen had participated in preparing for the December 1965 world congress, just a few months after the Indonesian catastrophe. Hansen was in the hospital in Paris and unable to attend the congress, however, and the amendments adopted by the majority reversed its political line. When the SWP leadership learned of these changes following the congress, they wrote a protest to the United Secretariat:

> Since receiving the final draft of the resolution on the Sino-Soviet conflict, on February 21, . . . we have held a number of discussions on the problem that was created for us, by the considerable modifications that were introduced into the draft submitted to the congress.
>
> The most significant changes involve the characterization of the Mao leadership. In the draft resolution, the Mao leadership was held to come under the general category of Stalinism although with peculiarities of its own due to the influence of the Chinese revolution. The direction of the changes introduced into the draft resolution was to

substitute for this a characterization of the Mao leadership as left centrist.[2]

As it turned out, the lessons of the bloodbath in Indonesia and of the devastating bureaucratic social convulsions during the "Cultural Revolution" in China did *not* result in a narrowing of political differences in the leadership of the Fourth International. The record of this widening political divergence is fully documented in: *Discussion on China (1968–1971)*, an *International Information Bulletin* produced by the SWP in the early 1970s; and *International Internal Discussion Bulletin* no. 13 in 1973, which contains the draft resolution "Two Assessments of the Chinese Cultural Revolution: A Balance Sheet," submitted to the 1974 world congress by, among others, Joseph Hansen, Jack Barnes, Mary-Alice Waters, and Alan Harris.[3]

The debate took form around a resolution on the "Cultural Revolution" drafted by SWP leaders Joseph Hansen and George Novack, initially in consultation with Ernest Mandel, in preparation for the 1969 world congress. Once again, as in 1965, the line of the draft resolution was reversed through a series of amendments, this time submitted by Mandel, Pierre Frank, and Livio Maitan at a meeting of the United Secretariat prior to the congress. To clarify the differences, the SWP leadership prepared the draft resolution and the proposed amendments in dual columns—a painstaking labor that computer technology would make substantially simpler (although perhaps less visually effective) today! The resolution in this dual-column format can be found in both the above-mentioned internal bulletins, which some comrades in the Communist League undoubtedly have and that can be photocopied for comrades who want to read these documents. The collection *Discussion on China (1968–1971)* also contains Hansen's reports on this aspect of the 1969 world congress to the June 11 and June 18 New York City branch meetings and to the August 29–September 1 SWP convention.[4]

In the very first paragraph of the resolution drafted by Hansen and Novack, the modifier "Stalinized" was deleted from the description of the Chinese Communist Party—and the amendments continued in that political vein throughout. The issues in dispute were summarized as follows at the opening of the balance sheet submitted to the subsequent 1974 world congress:

> Those who spoke [in 1969] for the Maitan-Mandel-Frank amendments argued that while the Cultural Revolution had begun as an intrabureaucratic struggle, it had developed into something else. Mao and his followers, they contended, were sensitive to mass pressure for reforms. They said that significant concessions to the masses would be forthcoming as a result of the Cultural Revolution despite the bureaucratic character of the Mao faction. They regarded Maoist foreign policy as eclectic and inconsistent, wavering between opportunism in some countries and objectively anti-imperialist or revolutionary positions in others. The supporters of this resolution rejected the view that Mao would favor rapprochement with American imperialism at the expense of the world revolution.
>
> Those who favored the original resolution also viewed the Cultural Revolution as an intrabureaucratic struggle, but insisted that neither of the contenders would make major concessions to the masses. The supporters of this position held that Mao's policy on the international plane was fundamentally opportunist, aimed at reaching an accommodation with American imperialism and at practicing class collaboration with the bourgeoisie in the colonial and semicolonial countries.
>
> Underlying these two opposing views was a disagreement on the character of the Chinese Communist Party. The amendments

---

2. Quoted in "The Anatomy of Stalinism" in *The Mao Myth and the Legacy of Stalinism in China*, by Tom Kerry (Pathfinder, 1977), p. 157.

3. The balance sheet is reprinted in these pages. Joseph Hansen was the main drafter of this resolution. It was submitted by the members or fraternal members of the United Secretariat of the Fourth International who were leaders of the Leninist-Trotskyist Tendency: Abel (Art Young, Canada) and Adair (Alan Harris, United Kingdom), as well as fraternal members from the United States, Juan (Joseph Hansen), Hans (Jack Barnes), Pedro (Peter Camejo), Stateman (Barry Sheppard), and Thérèse (Mary-Alice Waters).

4. The dual-column resolution and reports by Hansen are reprinted in these pages.

proposed by Comrades Maitan, Mandel, and Frank showed that they considered it to be "bureaucratic centrist," i.e., that under the pressure of the masses or in resisting imperialism the Maoists could occasionally be expected to take positions close to those of revolutionary Marxism.

The original document analyzed the policies of the Maoists—socialism in one country, the two-stage theory of revolution, zigzags in pursuit of peaceful coexistence, opposition to proletarian democracy—as expressions of the interests of a "crystallized bureaucratic caste" that ought properly to be called Stalinist because of its essential similarity to the counterrevolutionary bureaucracy consolidated in the Soviet Union in the 1920s and 1930s.

Most important, as Hansen concluded in his report to the 1969 New York City branch meetings:

> [L]ooming behind all of these differences is the question of how to go about building a revolutionary combat party. In the United States, this concerns us a great deal. We see it in relation not only to the Communist party, which is no longer the great problem it once was, but in relation to the ultraleftism of [the Maoist] Progressive Labor [party], of tendencies in the SDS [Students for a Democratic Society] and other formations, notably the Black Panthers. We have the impression that other sectors of the world Trotskyist movement face comparable problems in their daily work of forging a combat party.
>
> The amendments to the original resolution pointed to actions by the Chinese CP that "objectively favored anti-imperialist struggles in various parts of the world, especially Southeast Asia, the Arab countries and Africa." The balance sheet by Barnes, Hansen, Harris, Waters, et al responded:
>
> This statement did not withstand the test of events. Even at the time it was written, the memory was still fresh of the debacle in Indonesia in 1965 in which as many as several hundred thousand members and supporters of the pro-Maoist Indonesian CP were slaughtered as the price of that party's Peking-approved prostration before the Sukarno regime.
>
> The balance sheet also pointed to the example of the workers and peasants government in Algeria, where "Peking for its own factional reasons was the first government in the world to recognize the reactionary Boumedienne regime after the coup that overthrew Ben Bella in June 1965." Only a few months after this 1973 balance sheet was issued, Peking was also among the first governments in the world to recognize the bloody fascist-like dictatorship in Chile, slamming the door of its embassy in Santiago in the face of refugees from Pinochet's reign of terror.

My aim in this note is not to review all the political questions taken up in these and other publications of our world movement. But these handful of references alone should shed some further light on statements in Mandel's article such as, "The leaders of the PKI [Indonesian CP] did not assimilate these lessons of history"—or a sentence not included in the *Militant* excerpt: "Underlying this erroneous tactic [of blocking mass actions by workers and peasants "aiming at the conquest of power"] is a false theoretical concept of the conditions for victory in the colonial revolution and of the nature of the state. . . ."

But responsibility for the defeat lay not with bad ideas, but with the self-serving class-collaborationist course of the privileged bureaucratic caste in Peking and its subservient followers in the leadership of the Indonesian Communist Party. Only by clearly understanding the accountability of Stalinism for the 1965 catastrophe in Indonesia can we accurately appreciate the historic significance of the fact—underlined by Ma'mud in his letter to the *Militant*—that the Indonesian workers, peasants, and youth who are today beginning to return to political life no longer confront this massive counterrevolutionary obstacle that repeatedly stood in their path to victory throughout much of this century.

As class-struggle developments unfold such as those in Indonesia and the broader "Asian crisis," all of us—individually and collectively—will act with greater political self-confidence and effectiveness if we do the disciplined work to ground what we are doing and what we are saying in the hard-won revolutionary continuity of the working class.

In this regard, possibly, communists can be considered deeply conservative—a trait we emulate from Lenin, who never failed to test his political judgments against the class-struggle experience generalized in the works of Marx and Engels for the use of current and future generations of proletarian fighters. There is no better source of this written record of struggle than the books, pamphlets, and periodicals the communist movement is now reaching out to our members and supporters the world over to help us keep in print.

Comradely,

s/ Steve Clark
Steve Clark
for the Political Committee

INTRODUCTION TO 'THE CATASTROPHE IN INDONESIA'
by Joseph Hansen

The three documents reprinted here as a pamphlet[1] deal with a defeat to the world socialist revolution—a major defeat that is still reverberating in world politics. The documents attempt to analyze the defeat and to draw some critical lessons from it.

It is quite fashionable among revolutionists to talk about the need for criticism and self-criticism in relation to setbacks to their cause. Unfortunately the breach between acknowledgment of the need and actually carrying it out is a wide one.

There are a number of reasons for this.

First of all, the struggle for socialism is a difficult one. Of all the great tasks which humanity has faced in the slow upward climb from savagery and barbarism toward genuine civilization, the battle to overcome capitalism and to establish planned economy on a world scale is undoubtedly the most toilsome and complicated single undertaking. To compensate for this, there exists a strong tendency to concentrate on the heartening signs, the successes, that prove that progress is indeed being made. The other side of this is a readiness to offset the demoralizing consequences of serious setbacks by excluding the real situation from consciousness.

These psychological reflexes are given strong and often quite deliberate reinforcement by the narrow-minded or self-seeking bureaucracies to be found in many working-class organizations. Conservative trade-union bureaucrats prefer to completely ignore defeats like the one in Indonesia when they do not actually cheer the crushing of "Communism." But opportunistic leaders of political parties whose programs are ostensibly dedicated to socialism are just as guilty. The most pernicious are those who claim to stand in the tradition of Leninism but who have converted *criticism*—the application of ruthlessly objective analysis—into a mere ritual that aims at covering up and even prettifying costly and damaging setbacks to the workers' movement.

In the case of Indonesia, neither the Kremlin nor Peking has offered even a ritualistic simulacrum. An entire year has passed since the disaster that shattered the largest Communist party in the capitalist world, yet not a single attempt, however superficial, has been made by either of the centers to analyze what went wrong and why.

Certainly sufficient resources are available to both governments to make such an analysis. Moscow has proved its capacity to secure first-rate photographs of the other side of the moon and Peking has recently provided most convincing proof of its capacity to produce a hydrogen deterrent to war. Surely either of them, or both of them combined, should be able to crack the secret that enabled a handful of reactionary generals in a backward country to overcome a huge mass party able to count on the experience and advice of both Peking and Moscow!

It requires no James Bond or Superintendent Maigret to discover why Mao and Khrushchev's heirs are not vying in the field of analyzing the defeat in Indonesia. The policy of each is to say nothing. To put it bluntly, they have a tacit agreement not to probe into this delicate area where the only real difference concerns which was most to blame.

---

1. This piece by Joseph Hansen originally appeared as the introduction to a 1966 pamphlet *The Catastrophe in Indonesia* published by Merit Publishers, the predecessor of Pathfinder. See "Maoism vs. Bolshevism: Letter to a comrade in the United Kingdom" by Steve Clark, reprinted earlier in this Education for Socialists publication, for a discussion on the contents and history of the pamphlet.

For revolutionists—and much broader circles!—it is nonetheless a vital matter, even a life and death matter, to understand serious defeats and how they could have been prevented. Thus in Indonesia, it was precisely the lack of widespread understanding of the defeats and setbacks suffered by the socialist revolution in the twenties and thirties, and again in the postwar period in Europe, that paved the way for another debacle comparable to the one suffered by the workers of Germany at the hands of Hitler in the early thirties.

And it is precisely because the working class generally still does not understand the role played by Stalinism in the events leading to World War II that the world today stands at the brink of a nuclear conflict.

The series of defeats in a number of countries, above all in Germany, gave the imperialists in the mid-thirties the conviction that they could plunge into a world war without thereby signing a death warrant for capitalism. They were confirmed in their belief by what happened in the civil war in Spain where Stalin, to prove to imperialism his capacity to play the role of savior of their system and thereby win for the Kremlin at least forbearance from attack, deliberately blocked a socialist victory. Spain, as Leon Trotsky pointed out at the time, constituted the "last warning" for humanity; inasmuch as the imperialist powers, by intervening in the civil war, were converting Spain into a proving ground for World War II.

Today the course of the conflict in Vietnam offers many striking parallels to the tragedy in Spain. Not the least of these is the parallel between the defeat in Germany and the defeat in Indonesia. The events in Indonesia can be glossed over only at risk of paying a most fearful price!

In analyzing what happened in Indonesia, it is possible to make a serious mistake in methodology. This is to confine the analysis to the Indonesian scene alone, leaving out the international context. Such an error would emphasize what is peculiar to the archipelago and tend to obscure the general pattern that applies to other countries as well. It would likewise tend to isolate Indonesia from the overall context of international events and block an understanding of the reciprocal play of cause and effect on a world scale.

To fully appreciate the enormity of the debacle in Indonesia, it is necessary, for instance, to see it as the culmination of a series of setbacks that occurred after the colonial revolution reached a high point with the victory of the Cuban Revolution in 1959. The immediate consequence of the triumph in Cuba was to provide fresh inspiration and hope to the masses throughout the colonial world. This was particularly visible in the upsurge in the Congo and elsewhere in Africa, as in Algeria and Zanzibar.

Then a series of setbacks occurred, some due to adventuristic actions associated with a wrong appreciation or wrong application of the lessons of the Cuban victory, some due—and this was much the more decisive and widespread—to class-collaborationist, "peaceful coexistence" policies.

In one country after another, the military caste seized power in coup d'états and proceeded to crush or drive underground the revolutionary movements seeking an agrarian reform, national liberation, a planned economy. The biggest defeat before the one in Indonesia occurred in Brazil in April 1964. Other sharp setbacks occurred in the Congo and Algeria, to name but the most prominent. Since the defeat in Indonesia, Ghana has been added to the list.

In brief, the series of defeats in a number of other countries in the colonial world increased the potentiality for a defeat in Indonesia.

Thus, instead of being provided with a new example like Cuba—one that would serve both to provide fresh inspiration to the masses and also a model more applicable perhaps to conditions in their own country—the Indonesian masses were confronted with a series of depressing setbacks.

It was all the more important, therefore, for the leaders of the Chinese Communist party to play a positive role and to do their utmost to help put the Indonesian Communist party on the right track. The Chinese Revolution had enormous impact on the Indonesian masses, as it did on the masses throughout the colonial world. The successes and achievements of planned economy in China—despite the errors and limitations—further impressed the masses, especially when viewed against the continued stagnation and decay in countries like India where capitalism still prevails. The credit due the Chinese Revolution thus redounded to the leaders of the Chinese Communist party, lending extraordinary authority to their attitudes and advice.

But the policy of the Mao leadership was to cover up and even foster the opportunism of the Aidit group in the Indonesian Communist party. Thus in relation to Indonesia, Mao played a role comparable to that of Stalin in the German events. Just as Stalin, out of passing diplomatic needs, blocked the German Communist party from developing a revolutionary policy that could have stopped Hitler and put the German working class in power, so Mao out of similar passing diplomatic needs (an alliance with Sukarno and the Indonesian bourgeoisie) blocked the Indonesian Communist party from developing a revolutionary policy that could have stopped the reactionary generals and put the Indonesian working class in power.

Clearly, the defeat in Indonesia cannot be understood without understanding how and why the Indonesian masses turned towards China and how and why it was possible for Peking to play such a pernicious role in turning these same masses away from the road to victory.

If the connection between the defeats in other countries and the defeat in Indonesia is ill understood, this holds all the more so for the international repercussions that followed upon the defeat.

In Vietnam the struggle of the freedom fighters at once became ten times more difficult.

A victory in Indonesia would have meant a great new powerful ally in the camp of the workers' states. It needs little to visualize how this would have affected the popular mood in the Soviet Union, Eastern Europe and China, compelling the governments of these countries to firm up their foreign policy. The pressure upon them to furnish adequate aid to the Vietnamese fighters, for instance, would have increased to irresistible proportions. A revolutionary government in Indonesia would itself have intervened directly in Moscow and Peking along these lines, not to mention the aid it would have mobilized in consonance with its own immediate interests to beat back the thrust of American imperialism in Southeast Asia.

Instead of this, the defeat in Indonesia acted as a new depressant on the Vietnamese freedom fighters. That they have maintained their struggle as valiantly as they have *despite this* shows how heroic they really are.

The defeat in Indonesia also had grave repercussions for the colonial revolution, the workers' states and the socialist struggle in general through the encouragement it provided the most belligerent sectors of the American ruling class—those that want to get on with the grandiose scheme of spreading their empire until it girdles the globe. The physical liquidation of the Indonesian Communist party deprived Johnson of one of his main arguments for intervening in the civil war in Vietnam; namely, the argument that if the U.S. did not shore up the Saigon regime it would fall and that would mean a whole role of dominoes going down. By way of compensation, the victory of the ultrareactionary coup d'état in Indonesia greatly strengthened the position of the U. S. armed forces in Southeast Asia and thereby reduced the risk inherent in further escalation of the war in Vietnam.

The ultimate consequences of the defeat in Indonesia can thus be seen in the flow of American casualties from Vietnam and the heightened danger of a nuclear catastrophe.

The most spectacular immediate result of the defeat in Indonesia, however, is to be seen in China. The evidence strongly indicates that it was the precipitating cause for the "cultural revolution" which has so surprised and puzzled the Sinologists.

It is rather broadly understood that Mao's ultraleft extremism led to Peking's isolation among the workers' states and Communist parties. To openly reject a united front against the military aggression of American imperialism in Vietnam with governments, parties and groupings that do not meet with Mao's full approval could obviously end only with the Chinese Communist party standing alone; and with the blame pinned on it, moreover, for making a common front impossible. This in turn had the effect of strengthening Khrushchevism, the pernicious continuation of Stalinism. It is not so widely understood that Mao's opportunism with regard to Sukarno and the Indonesian Communist party had similar results. A major ally, the Indonesian Communist party, was smashed; Indonesia was converted from a friendly country into an enemy power; the aggressive designs of American imperialism were given fresh impetus; and China's defenses were greatly weakened by these shifts on the international scene.

There is considerable evidence to show that these results of Mao's foreign policy caused great concern to a broad spectrum of leaders in the Chinese government and the bureaucracy as a whole. The criticisms that were voiced, even if muffled or made indirectly, undoubtedly resounded throughout the country. The all too evident rise in the war danger demanded immediate consideration of the country's defenses.

Although rather long-standing differences over domestic policies evidently played a major role in the purges and turmoil that took place under the misleading label of a "cultural revolution," the timing as well as other attendant circumstances show that it was Mao's foreign policy, above all the disaster resulting from it in Indonesia, that touched off the internal conflict that has shaken China.

How the outcome of this conflict will ultimately affect the foreign policy of the Chinese government and how this in turn will enter into new events remains to be seen.

Lest the picture seem too dark, attention should be called to the major differences between the international setting today and the setting of the twenties and thirties.

First, the difference in level between the industrially backward and industrially advanced countries—which is the prime generator of the colonial revolution—continues to deepen. An inflationary process unremittingly cuts into the standard of living of the masses. This is coupled with extreme rigidity among the indigenous oligarchies with regard to concessions and reforms. The combination repeatedly packs fresh explosives into the rotted social structures of the colonial world.

Secondly, the examples provided by Russia, Eastern Europe, China and Cuba in showing a practical alternative to capitalist stagnation are now so deeply engraved in popular consciousness as to be ineradicable among the masses in all the underdeveloped countries.

These two main factors explain one of the new features in world politics today—the quickness with which the masses recover from defeats that formerly would have left them prostrate for decades.

To this must be added the shattering of the Stalinist monolith and the appearance of new revolutionary currents such as Castroism. Both phenomena, which are of course interrelated, greatly facilitate finding a solution to the key problem of building a leadership capable of winning power.

There is thus every reason for taking an optimistic stand and holding out the expectation that the vanguard of the working class will succeed in meeting the great historic challenge. It will create the political mechanism required to assure fresh victories of the socialist revolution. It will do it in time to prevent a third world war.

One of the necessary conditions for reversing the string of defeats and opening up a series of victories is to broaden the vanguard's understanding of the meaning of the defeats, above all the major ones like the debacle in Indonesia. This pamphlet is intended to help in carrying out that task.

On the documents themselves, a word should be added as to authorship. Ernest Mandel is the editor of the Belgian socialist weekly *La Gauche*. He has written extensively on political and economic subjects of interest to the revolutionary socialist movement. His book *Traité d'Économie Marxiste* won him a firm reputation throughout Europe as a Marxist economist. An English edition of this important work is now in preparation.

The second document is by the United Secretariat of the Fourth International. This is the leading body of the world party of socialist revolution founded by Leon Trotsky in 1938. As a statement of position on an important contemporary event, the document is indicative of how well the Fourth International stands in the tradition established by its founder.

The third document was written by a young member of the Indonesian Communist party who succeeded in making his way into exile. His analysis of Aidit's policies is of the greatest interest not only in the material it provides as a guide for further study but as an indication of the determination of an important sector of the Indonesian Communist party to learn from what happened and to utilize the lessons in such a way as to ensure victory when the masses again surge forward, as they surely will.

NOVEMBER 28, 1966

TWO ASSESSMENTS OF THE CHINESE CULTURAL REVOLUTION: A BALANCE SHEET
Draft Resolution for the Fourth World Congress Since Reunification
Submitted by United Secretariat members Abel, Adair, Hans, Juan, Pedro, Stateman and Therese

I. THE TWO LINES AT THE 1969 WORLD CONGRESS AND THE TEST OF EVENTS

Prior to the last world congress, the Fourth International, in several meetings of the United Secretariat and of the International Executive Committee, as well as in its press and in the international discussion bulletins, began analyzing the so-called Cultural Revolution unfolding in China. (The public part of this analysis is available in the back issues of *Quatrième Internationale* and *Intercontinental Press*. The internal discussion, published in English in the International Information Bulletin *Discussion on China* [1968–1971], is not yet available in other languages.)

The United Secretariat decided to place the discussion of the Cultural Revolution on the agenda of the Third World Congress Since Reunification (Ninth World Congress), and asked the Political Committee of the Socialist Workers Party to prepare a draft resolution as the basis for discussion.

This was written by Comrades George Novack and Joseph Hansen, after consultation with Comrade Ernest Mandel. It drew heavily on the analyses made by Comrades Chen Pi-lan and the IEC member of the Chinese section of the Fourth International, Peng Shu-tse, who had written extensively on the Chinese Cultural Revolution. (See *The Chinese Revolution, Part III*, Education for Socialists bulletin, by Comrades Chen and Peng.)

In light of the discussion with Comrade Mandel, the SWP Political Committee assumed that the draft resolution would be adopted unanimously, with perhaps alterations of an editorial nature. However, a majority of those present at the meeting of the United Secretariat where the draft was considered found that they disagreed with the line. Comrades Maitan, Mandel, and Frank took the lead in proposing amendments of such nature as to change the basic analysis and orientation of the resolution. The amended version was adopted by a majority of the United Secretariat. (Both versions, arranged in dual columns so that the changes can easily be followed, are reprinted at the end of this resolution. See "Draft resolution on the Cultural Revolution in dual columns," pp. 27–48.)

At the world congress Comrade Maitan reported for the United Secretariat majority on the resolution containing the Maitan-Mandel-Frank amendments. Comrade Ross Dowson reported on the original Peng-Novack-Hansen resolution. The vote was divided, the Maitan-Mandel-Frank resolution receiving a majority.

Comrade Peng was granted extended time to express his tactical differences on the attitude taken in both documents toward the Liu Shao-chi oppositionists. In his opinion, the Fourth International should have offered critical support to Liu Shao-chi against Mao's purge in order to better reach open-minded Chinese militants with the program of Trotskyism.

Peng argued that the Fourth International should have adopted a more interventionist approach toward the Cultural Revolution. In a statement accompanying his vote for the original resolution, he indicated that the discussion of the Cultural Revolution had already become a historical question inasmuch as the decisive defeat of Liu Shao-chi by the Maoists marked the end of this stage of the upheaval in China. The most important thing to be accomplished by the world congress in its discussion of China, he said, was "to clarify the theoretical differences in order to prepare for the future."

Comrades Moreno and Lorenzo of Argentina had not seen the resolutions prior to the congress—

they were not available in Spanish—and thus had not had time to study them. Consequently they did not vote for either of the resolutions placed before the delegates. They submitted a brief written statement expressing their view on the character of the Chinese student movement, which they placed in the framework of the worldwide youth radicalization as a precursor of political revolution in China. This statement suggested defining the Cultural Revolution "as a highly contradictory phenomenon characterized by . . . the manipulation and utilization, by the Mao faction of the bureaucracy, of the Chinese student movement, in order to overcome the grave crisis in which the bureaucratic caste and Chinese society found themselves, and in order thereby to save that same bureaucratic caste represented by Mao from the inevitable struggle of the Chinese masses against it, through a political revolution."

They deferred further analysis until they and the rest of the leadership of the Argentine section had an opportunity to study the documentation.

The issues in dispute

In the light of the events since 1969 it should now be possible to draw a definitive balance sheet on the differences expressed in the two resolutions.

The disputed points on the Chinese Cultural Revolution concerned both the foreign and domestic policy of the People's Republic of China. Those who spoke for the Maitan-Mandel-Frank amendments argued that while the Cultural Revolution had begun as an intrabureaucratic struggle, it had developed into something else. Mao and his followers, they contended, were sensitive to mass pressure for reforms. They said that significant concessions to the masses would be forthcoming as a result of the Cultural Revolution despite the bureaucratic character of the Mao faction. They regarded Maoist foreign policy as eclectic and inconsistent, wavering between opportunism in some countries and objectively anti-imperialist or revolutionary positions in others. The supporters of this resolution rejected the view that Mao would favor rapprochement with American imperialism at the expense of the world revolution.

Those who favored the original resolution also viewed the Cultural Revolution as an intrabureaucratic struggle, but insisted that neither of the contenders would make major concessions to the masses. The supporters of this position held that Mao's policy on the international plane was fundamentally opportunist, aimed at reaching an accommodation with American imperialism and at practicing class collaboration with the bourgeoisie in the colonial and semicolonial countries.

Underlying these two opposing views was a disagreement on the character of the Chinese Communist Party. The amendments proposed by Comrades Maitan, Mandel, and Frank showed that they considered it to be "bureaucratic centrist," i.e., that under the pressure of the masses or in resisting imperialism the Maoists could occasionally be expected to take positions close to those of revolutionary Marxism.

The original document analyzed the policies of the Maoists—socialism in one country, the two-stage theory of revolution, zigzags in pursuit of peaceful coexistence, opposition to proletarian democracy—as expressions of the interests of a "crystallized bureaucratic caste" that ought properly to be called Stalinist because of its essential similarity to the counterrevolutionary bureaucracy consolidated in the Soviet Union in the 1920s and 1930s.

More specific differences concerned (1) the degree of independence of the Red Guards from the Maoist apparatus; (2) whether the army became the predominant organized force in the government in the course of the fight with Liu Shao-chi; (3) whether the Cultural Revolution had extended or further restricted the democratic rights of the Chinese masses; (4) whether Peking's criticisms of the Kremlin contributed to the growth of left oppositional currents in the Soviet Union and Eastern Europe.

Both resolutions included the following paragraph on the situation at the outbreak of the Cultural Revolution in 1966:

"The high officials around Liu apparently sought to close ranks against Mao following the disastrous results of the Great Leap Forward. Liu and his close associates took fright at the appalling consequences of this adventure, counseled retreat, and succeeded in switching over to a more prudent economic course. During this readjustment, the Liu grouping took control of the party apparatus and pushed Mao to one side. . . .

"By 1965 Mao felt that he was in position to break Liu's hold upon the regime and regain his lost supremacy. By exploiting his immense prestige, by maneuvering between the diverse tendencies and cutting them down one after another, by slandering Liu and his men through a relentless propaganda campaign, Mao succeeded in isolating them and eroding their bases of support among the masses, in the party, the army and the provinces and completing their downfall." (*Discussion on China* [1969–1971], pp. 29–30.)

The amended resolution, however, adduced a further reason for Mao's course:

"The 'cultural revolution' constitutes objectively an attempt by the Mao faction to divert the social forces pushing in that direction [i.e., toward a political revolution] from an overthrow of the bureaucracy into a reform of the bureaucracy." (Ibid., p.27.)

Mao's 'concessions'

The estimate that Mao intended to offer concessions to the masses was one of the themes advanced by Comrades Maitan, Mandel, and Frank. Its corollary was the assumption that the Red Guard and workers mobilizations represented an upsurge from below, largely independent of either wing of the bureaucracy, to which the Maoist wing was more responsive.

While the original draft, for instance, described the mobilizations of the masses as "limited and episodic" (p. 31), the word "episodic" was deleted from the amended draft. The original draft included two paragraphs (pp. 32 and 33) stressing the "tendency of the Red Guards toward conformism"; these, too, were deleted. The original draft described the "revolutionary committees" set up by the Maoists to exercise power locally as composed of "individuals handpicked by the authorities" (p. 35). This phrase was removed, the substitution being the view that the "revolutionary committees" were constituted "by compromise between contending factions." Sections on the cultural sterility of the Cultural Revolution were likewise deleted, along with a comparison of the cult of Mao with that of Stalin (p. 36).

The original draft clearly stated the antidemocratic results of the Cultural Revolution:

"The 'cultural revolution' has ended in the constriction of democracy and the fortification of the positions of one faction of the bureaucracy against its rivals rather than the expansion and deepening of decision-making powers by the masses." (p. 38)

This paragraph was removed and replaced with one stressing a supposed "compromise between the Maoist faction and parts of the old majority faction." The "constriction of democracy" pointed to in the original draft was reduced to "an attempt to stop the mass movement and to restore a new form of bureaucratic rule. . . ."

The implication in the amended resolution that Mao stood, perhaps reluctantly, to the left of Liu Shao-chi on mobilizing the masses, establishing workers' democracy, and reforming the bureaucracy has not been borne out by the events. Nor has the assumption that the Cultural Revolution ended in a compromise between the two factions rather than in a consolidation of Mao's authoritarian rule.

To the degree that elements of the bureaucratically created Red Guards did move outside the prescribed framework as an instrument of Mao's purge they were ruthlessly crushed by the regime and deported to the countryside. Neither in economic policy nor in the administration of the so-called revolutionary committees have significant improvements in the standard of living of the masses or in their democratic rights been registered in the years since the end of the Cultural Revolution.

In the fall of 1971, following the purge of Lin Piao, a campaign was opened against "ultraleftism." This was directed at those who opposed the reinstating of lower-level party functionaries removed during the Cultural Revolution, and at those who continued to call for reductions in the pay of administrators and officials demagogically promised on a number of occasions by the Maoists during the fight against Liu Shao-chi.

The youth remain a special target of the Maoist regime. It has been seven years since China's universities were closed during the Cultural Revolution. Most of them reopened with sharply reduced admissions in mid-1970. Today there are only a fourth as many university students in China as there were in 1966 and these are overwhelmingly members of the ruling party or of its youth organization of unquestioned loyalty to the regime.

The deportation of educated youth to the countryside continues unabated. A September 15–16, 1972, Hsinhua dispatch reported:

"Millions of educated youth from the cities have settled down in mountainous areas and countryside since the Great Proletarian Cultural Revolution. They are maturing politically thanks to re-education by the poor and middle peasants."

The same dispatch reported, "400,000 educated young people have settled in the Chinese countryside since the beginning of this year."

The role of the army

Closely related to the differences over Mao's alleged concessions to the masses were the opposing assessments made by the two sides at the world congress on the relative importance of the People's Liberation Army (PLA) in setting the pattern for and enforcing the Cultural Revolution. Mao, confined to a minority in the party and governmental bureaucracy, enlisted outside forces to purge the Liuists. These were the Red Guards, which were most prominent between May 1966 and January 1967, and Lin Piao's PLA, which replaced the Red Guards as the principal instrument of Maoist power in January 1967.

In keeping with what it considered to be the "bureaucratic centrist" nature of Maoist policies and the independent role of the masses and Red Guards during the Cultural Revolution, Comrades Maitan, Mandel, and Frank took a position different from that of Comrades Peng, Novack, and Hansen on the centralization of power in military hands in the course of the purge of Liu Shao-chi. This is evident in several places in the two documents. Where the original draft stressed "the role of the army under Lin Piao as ultimate authority" (p. 31), the amended draft reads "increased authority of the army under Lin Piao." The original draft further stated:

"However much the military high command has been shaken and its leadership divided over the past period, an ominous pattern has been set for the future." (p. 32)

This was removed and in its place a sentence added reading:

"However, Mao tends to reduce again this great weight gained by the army during the previous period, by putting the emphasis on the reconstruction of the party as the mainstay of the regime and the necessity of a single central leadership for all power apparatuses."

This was written just before the Ninth Congress of the Chinese CP elected a Central Committee composed 40 percent of army officers, and two years before the last of the provincial "revolutionary committees" had been established, in which twenty-one of the twenty-six provincial and municipal administrations were dominated by the PLA.

The strength and influence of the military, far from decreasing after 1969, was on the upswing. The danger became so acute that Mao felt forced to eliminate Lin Piao and a number of other high military officials in 1971. The Cultural Revolution thus ended in a knockdown fight between Mao and his constitutionally designated heir, who had served as the main instrument in carrying out the purge of Liu Shao-chi. This was almost two-and-a-half years after Peng, Novack, and Hansen had proposed calling attention to this "ominous pattern" in a resolution of the Fourth International.

The purge of Lin Piao marked a further narrowing of the bureaucratic center in Peking. In addition to Lin and other top military leaders who disappeared, Chen Po-ta, Mao's longtime personal secretary and a guiding light of the Cultural Revolution, was eliminated from the leadership.

Today virtually all the old leaders of the CCP have been eliminated. Of the twenty-one members of the Politburo put together by Mao at the Ninth Party Congress in April 1969, eleven have disappeared or died. Of the five members of the Standing Committee of the Politburo, the highest decision-making body in China, only Mao and Chou En-lai remain.

The inability of this Stalinist leadership to renew its ranks, even from within its own apparatus, is further evidence of the correctness of the estimate in the original resolution that the Cultural Revolution aimed at further centralization and narrowing of the bureaucratic hierarchy, not its democratization. From its earliest days in power the CCP Central Committee and Politburo have been distrustful of new leaders. The "old guard" jealously clung to its power and prerogatives. It functioned as a tight-knit clique that has grown smaller and more ossified with the attrition of age. Mao's Cultural Revolution sought to displace this grouping with his personal dictatorship, not to broaden its base. This was clear in the choice of leaders at the Ninth Party Congress. Of the twenty-one members elected to the Politburo at that time, the average age was sixty-eight. Only one member was under fifty. There have been no additions to the leadership since then, only new purges. Mao himself will be eighty in December, and the few loyal subordinates he permits to retain positions of authority are almost without exception of the same generation, constituting the most aged ruling body of any regime in the world.

The process we have witnessed parallels Stalin's purges of his own faction in the later Moscow Trials, after he had eliminated all oppositions that represented fundamental differences of line. Before the Cultural Revolution and the fall of Lin, Mao's authority rested at least technically on the collective agreement of the Stalinist clique that spoke in the name of the Chinese Communist Party. Now, the relations have been reversed and the ultimate authority in all matters is the Bonapartist octogenarian. This was the position finally consolidated by Stalin in the Soviet Union after the Moscow Trials and his purge of the Red Army leadership in 1938.

Peaceful coexistence, detente with Nixon, and Vietnam

The validity of the position stated in the original resolution was borne out even more dramatically with regard to the possibility of a detente between Mao and Nixon. Fresh evidence of Mao's basic foreign policy was at hand when the two versions of the Cultural Revolution document were drafted. In November 1968, Chinese officials had called for a resumption of talks in Warsaw with representatives of the incoming Nixon administration for the purpose of establishing "peaceful coexistence" with Washington.

Because of their view that Maoism is a "centrist" formation, Comrades Maitan, Mandel, and Frank discounted this diplomatic move. The original draft had stated:

"The bankruptcy of this [Mao's] foreign policy became glaringly clear when, after deposing Liu Shao-chi as a 'lackey of imperialism, modern revisionism and the Kuomintang reactionaries,' Mao offered 'peaceful coexistence' to the Nixon administration." (pp. 28–29)

This sentence was removed from the document. It was replaced with the following:

"It can even not be excluded that a change of line of U. S. imperialism towards China would lead to a significant modification of revolutionary militancy advised by the Chinese leadership to its followers abroad—a normalization of relations at state level with the USA being in itself of course not reprehensible."

This forecast turned out to be wrong. It assumed that Mao's basic foreign policy was not to actively seek a deal with U.S. imperialism. It assumed that Mao and his followers abroad were in general acting with "revolutionary militancy" in mind rather than in accordance with the narrow national interests of the Peking bureaucracy; and that what was involved was the "normalization" of diplomatic relations, which at worst might lead to modification of Mao's "revolutionary" advice to his followers abroad.

Normalization of diplomatic relations was of course not reprehensible in itself. But that was not all that Mao and Nixon projected. Besides ending the U.S. embargo against China, with its concomitants of admission to the United Nations, the opening of trade, and diplomatic recognition, Mao wanted an understanding that would slow down any aggressive military plans of the Soviet Union. In return Mao was prepared to show Nixon that he could be relied on every bit as much as Stalin or Brezhnev to aid in maintaining the international status quo by opposing revolutions.

The real stake for Nixon was Vietnam. Mao paid off by inviting Nixon to Peking in February 1972. So that the Vietnamese should be certain not to miss the point, Nixon timed his visit to Peking to coincide with a savage escalation of the bombing of Indochina. Mao and Chou issued a polite rebuke and went ahead with the gala reception of the imperialist chieftain. The warm welcome given Nixon proved an invaluable boost to his prospects for reelection and thus strengthened his hand in wringing concessions from the beleaguered Vietnamese and demobilizing the worldwide antiwar movement. It absolved in advance Brezhnev's new betrayal of the Vietnamese at the subsequent summit meeting in Moscow.

On May 8, 1972, Nixon announced the mining of Haiphong harbor and the bombardment of rail links with China—two moves that the Pentagon had feared to take throughout the Vietnam war because of the danger of finally provoking a response from Moscow and Peking. Neither the Soviet Union nor China replied to this monstrous escalation of the war. They did not mobilize their followers around the world to protest the American aggression. They made no show of force to compel Nixon to back down.

The Soviet Union still refused to supply North Vietnam with the sophisticated missiles and aircraft that could have ended the American monopoly of the air over Indochina—equipment that had been supplied in abundance to the bourgeois government of Egypt. Moscow did not even cancel the summit meeting with Nixon a few weeks later. The outpouring of antiwar sentiment around the world after Nixon's May 8 action built toward potentially massive proportions. Then, under the impact of Moscow's and Peking's betrayal, it dissipated and fell back.

It was under these circumstances that the North Vietnamese and the Provisional Revolutionary Government undertook a forced retreat from their previous bargaining positions in Paris and accepted an accord in January 1973 that contained unfavorable clauses, leaving the Saigon regime intact and bolstered by a pledge not to attempt to overthrow it by military means.

In a statement issued in Peking on January 29, Mao Tse-tung, Chou En-lai, Tung Pi-wu, and Chu teh described the Paris agreement as "a great victory for the three Indochinese peoples' united struggle." (*Peking Review,* February 2, 1973.)

A further touch to Moscow and Peking's betrayal of the Vietnamese revolution came in the International Conference on Vietnam that concluded in Paris on March 2, 1973. There the Democratic Republic of Vietnam's "allies" pledged themselves to "guarantee" the American-imposed settlement. A Peking *People's Daily* editorial on March 3 hailed the conference and made this promise to Nixon:

"As a party to the Paris international conference and a signatory to its acts, China will seriously undertake the obligation to strictly implement the act of the Paris international conference and never do anything that hinders or violates the Paris agreement." (*Peking Review,* March 9, 1973.)

The agreement the Chinese Stalinists proudly proclaim themselves "a party to" explicitly recognizes the legitimacy of the Thieu regime, prohibits North Vietnamese aid to the struggle in the South, and legalizes American support to "the government set up after the general elections in South Vietnam provided for in Article 9," elections that if they are ever held at all will be conducted under Thieu's auspices in the most populous parts of the country.

The *People's Daily* editorial makes no mention of these onerous and dangerous conditions. Instead it asserts:

"The signing of the Paris agreement has put an end to the war in Vietnam." The Maoist regime, concerned above all else with building "socialism" within the borders of China, is prepared to barter the struggles of the oppressed everywhere else in exchange for a promise that China will be left alone.

Reason for the error

How did Comrades Maitan, Mandel, and Frank so badly misinterpret Mao's basic policy? How have they explained the events? And how do they explain the fact that the authors of the original resolution were able to make correct forecasts? Up to now they have not provided answers to these questions, although as responsible leaders it is their duty to do so.

Their mistakes flowed, it appears clear, from an incorrect judgment of the nature of the line being followed by Peking. They estimated Mao's attitude toward the world revolution as follows:

"The more radical line pursued by the Chinese leadership towards world revolutionary developments since the beginning of the Sino-Soviet conflict which, on several important questions, brought it nearer to the positions of revolutionary Marxism (an analysis confirmed in 1968 by Peking's attitude, in contrast to the Kremlin's, towards the May revolution in France, the prerevolutionary struggles in India, the Mexican students' struggles and the rising political revolution in the CSSR leading to the Warsaw Pact countries' occupation of Czechoslovakia), reflects both the specific relationship of imperialism and the Soviet bureaucracy toward the P.R. of China, and the objective impact of the rising tide of world revolution on the Chinese masses." (p. 28)

Comrade Maitan, the United Secretariat majority reporter, summarized his viewpoint clearly in the pre-Congress discussion as follows:

". . . But, despite the attitude of the Chinese in the Vietnamese affair, despite their responsibility in Indonesia, despite the lamentable bankruptcy of almost all the orthodox Maoist groups, we must not lose sight of:

"(a) That the international line of the Chinese remains objectively more progressive than the Soviet line and there is no ground for equating them.

"(b) That China is aiding and stimulating some sweeping guerrilla movements in several Asian countries.

"(c) That the Chinese criticism has had an incontestable effect in the revolutionary ripening of broad layers of the new revolutionary left in the advanced capitalist countries.

"(d) That despite certain traits of the 'cultural revolution,' the attitudes and conceptions of the Chinese leaders continue to operate objectively in a direction diametrically opposed to that of Stalinism. (The comrades will obviously understand that I am utilizing the term Stalinism here in the more specific sense of the word and not as a synonym for bureaucratic concepts and praxis in general)." (*An Insufficient Document,* reprinted IIB, *Discussion on Latin America* (1968–1972), p. 13.)

In the early years of the Sino-Soviet split the Fourth International took note of the fact that on several important points the positions voiced by Peking stood to the left of those upheld by the Kremlin. The Fourth International also fixed the blame on the Kremlin for precipitating the breach of relations between the two giant workers' states by unilaterally withdrawing its technicians and aid from China, which was and remains qualitatively more underdeveloped than the USSR. It was for these reasons that our movement critically supported Peking in its fight with the Kremlin. It was apparent as the Sino-Soviet dispute unfolded that what was involved on Peking's part was a turn toward bureaucratic ultraleftism and adventurism reminiscent of Third Period Stalinism, not a change of direction toward Marxist practice. Moreover, Peking simultaneously followed class-collaborationist policies with every bourgeois regime that responded favorably to its overtures.

To speak of Peking's "more radical line" in 1969, after the Indonesian catastrophe, was to overlook the practice of the Stalinist regime in Peking. The examples cited by Comrades Maitan, Mandel, and Frank where Peking's practice was allegedly to the left of the Kremlin's (France, India, Mexico, and Czechoslovakia) taken all together hardly outweigh the betrayal of the Indonesian revolution, still less the subsequent betrayal of Vietnam. In every case Mao's support remained largely verbal, his advice had an ultraleft sectarian character, and was dictated by considerations of factional advantage against the USSR, not by the needs of the revolutionary movement in the countries cited.

Maoism, the national bourgeoisie, and Maoist parties abroad

It is clear in retrospect that the authors of the amended resolution did not grasp the underlying consistency of Mao's peaceful coexistence policies and saw the betrayals in Indonesia and Pakistan as aberrations. Thus, where the original draft said clearly that "Mao followed a policy of collaborating with the colonial bourgeoisie, as in Pakistan," this was amended to read, "Mao followed in several countries a policy of collaborating with the colonial bourgeoisie. . . ." (p. 28)

The thesis that Maoist foreign policy was eclectic and only collaborationist in "several countries" was developed even more pointedly later in the resolution. The original draft contained the following paragraph:

"[Peking] has extended material aid to guerrilla forces as well as countries like Tanzania, thus helping to create an image far to the left of Moscow. Nevertheless, Peking's basic policy, as reiterated many times by its leaders and voiced once again upon the inauguration of the Nixon administration, has been 'peaceful coexistence' with U.S. imperialism. Out of narrow nationalistic considerations and in line with its doctrine that the revolution must first pass through a bourgeois stage before it can reach the socialist stage, Peking counsels and countenances support to bourgeois governments in Indonesia, Pakistan and other countries instead of mobilizing the masses for uncompromising struggle against the neocolonial regimes." (p. 39)

This assessment, the accuracy of which should be clear today, was replaced by some sentences extolling the "objectively" revolutionary contributions of Maoism throughout the world:

"[Peking] has extended material aid to guerrilla forces. This has not only created an image far to the left of Moscow but also objectively favored anti-imperialist struggles in various parts of the world, especially Southeast Asia, the Arab countries and Africa. Likewise, the sharp campaign which Peking unleashed against the right-wing opportunist line of the CP's following Moscow's lead, and against some key features of the bureaucratic rule in Eastern Europe, has objectively contributed to deepen the world crisis of Stalinism and to facilitate the upsurge of a new youth vanguard the world over."

This statment did not withstand the test of events. Even at the time it was written, the memory was still fresh of the debacle in Indonesia in 1965 in which as many as several hundred thousand members and supporters of the pro-Maoist Indonesian CP were slaughtered as the price of that party's Peking-approved prostration before the Sukarno regime. Mao later attempted to place the blame for this disaster on Liu Shao-chi, but there is ample evidence to prove that Mao gave his personal approval to the program and practice of the Indonesian CP. In a message of greetings to the Indonesian CP on May 20, 1965, scarcely four months before the bloodbath began, Mao praised the party and its leader, D. N. Aidit, for having "skillfully and creatively applied and developed Marxism-Leninism in the light of the revolutionary practice of its own country." (Hsinhua dispatch, May 23, 1965.)

In Algeria, Peking for its own factional reasons was the first government in the world to recognize the reactionary Boumedienne regime after the coup that overthrew Ben Bella in June 1965. In Latin America the verbal revolutionism of the Maoist sects covered Peking's growing uncritical support for "reformist" military dictatorships such as the Velasco government that seized power in Peru in October 1968.

Today hardly anyone in the world Trotskyist movement would argue that these were aberrations limited to "several countries" while on the whole Peking's foreign policy "objectively favored anti-imperialist struggles."

In 1971 the depth of Mao's commitment to peaceful coexistence received three separate tests in countries that maintained friendly relations with Peking. In each case China supported the counterrevolution. In March, Yahya Khan launched a bloodbath in East Bengal to prevent the Bengali people from freeing themselves from the national oppression they had suffered at the hands of their masters in West Pakistan. Peking denounced the separatist movement and continued to send aid to the military dictatorship.

In April the procapitalist Bandaranaike government in Ceylon sought to repress the rapidly growing organization of young radicals called the Janatha Vimukthi Peramuna (JVP—People's Liberation Front). Here, as in Pakistan, the Stalinists in Peking found themselves on the same side as American imperialism in providing aid to a counterrevolutionary regime engaged in a brutal repression of its own people.

The events in the Sudan in July, while receiving less international publicity than those in Ceylon and Bangladesh, were an equally clear demonstration of the counterrevolutionary policy of Peking. On July 19, General Nimeiry was overthrown by a military coup that received support from the Sudanese Communist Party, the largest CP in the Arab world.

Nimeiry returned to power in a countercoup on July 22 and proceeded to decimate the Sudanese CP and the trade unions. Radio Omdurman broadcast appeals to the population to denounce all "Communists, traitors to the fatherland, and enemies of God." By the end of the month the whole CP leadership was imprisoned and mass executions had begun. On August 5, Nimeiry sent a personal letter to Mao and Chou En-lai thanking them for supporting his regime in the crisis and refraining from condemning his witch-hunt.

In Africa, Peking openly endorses the "leftist" neocolonial regimes in Tanzania and Guinea. In Latin America it is pursuing not "armed struggle" but peaceful coexistence with governments throughout the continent with special stress on the popular front coalition headed by Salvador Allende in Chile.

The main thrust of Peking's political and diplomatic efforts in Europe is to secure recognition from the existing regimes, not to topple them. It has extended diplomatic recognition to and sought friendly relations with Franco's Spain and the Greece of the colonels. It openly endorses the Common Market as a progressive move by European imperialist powers aimed at the Soviet Union and the United States. It opposes reductions in NATO troop strength in Europe which might weaken capitalist Europe in face of the Soviet Union.

In Southeast Asia, Peking's betrayal of the Vietnamese revolution in exchange for improved relations with Washington is recognized by most of those who voted for the amended resolution submitted by the majority of the United Secretariat in 1969, although comrades Maitan, Mandel, and Frank insisted then on deleting any suggestion that such a thing could happen.

What remains of Peking's "objectively" anti-imperialist and revolutionary influence? Peking continues—as does the Kremlin—to mouth platitudes about anti-imperialist struggle. But in the last five years in the hot spots where it exerts influence it has either openly sided with the counterrevolution or covertly put pressure on those under fire to settle for peace at any price. The exceptions are few. They include the minimal support provided up to now to the guerrilla struggles in Burma and northern Thailand, countries on or near the Chinese border where from purely "buffer zone" considerations Peking can be expected to promote opposition to regimes in the orbit of American imperialism—until they come to terms with Chou En-lai.

Some of the sections or groups of the Fourth International have sought in their publications to explain this comprehensive policy of class collaboration as a "right turn" by Peking in response to concessions offered by American imperialism. This is wrong on two counts. First, it exaggerates the rightward shift in Peking's diplomacy since 1971 by down playing the earlier examples of such practice and the continuous professions by the Maoist leadership, even in its most ultraleft period, of a desire and willingness to secure peaceful coexistence with imperialism.

Second, it fails to grasp the fact that a generalized policy of peaceful coexistence is dictated by the material interests of the bureaucratic caste, which fears the spread of revolution and the effect it might have on the masses in its own country. The occasional turns toward adventurism taken by Stalinist bureaucrats, unlike the leftward vacillations of genuine centrists, have as their principal object applying pressure to imperialism to accept a mutual arrangement to maintain the status quo. They are not evidence of responsiveness to the revolutionary aspirations of the masses.

In one respect the Peking bureaucracy has shown itself to be even more narrowly nationalistic and provincial than its Stalinist counterpart in Moscow. That is in its indifference to the facade of international working class support that the Kremlin keeps up through its alliance with "fraternal parties" loyal to Moscow. Peking after some desultory efforts in 1960–67 to establish Maoist groups abroad, has abandoned any serious effort to penetrate the working-class movement in other countries.

Peking's international attention is now divided between expanding its ties with Washington and intensifying its efforts to use the United Nations as a forum to build a bloc of neocolonialist governments capable of maneuvering against the "superpowers"—the Soviet Union and the United States. Of the two superpowers, Peking openly labels the Soviet workers state as the "main enemy."

Peking and political revolution in Eastern Europe

In the amended resolution Comrades Maitan, Mandel, and Frank argued that "the sharp campaign which Peking unleashed against the rightwing opportunist line of the CPs following Moscow's lead, and against some key features of the bureaucratic rule in Eastern Europe, has objectively contributed to deepen the world crisis of Stalinism. . . ." (p. 39)

Many things, of course, "objectively" deepen the world crisis of Stalinism. Criticism of the Soviet bureaucracy by West European CPs under the pressure of Social Democracy have this effect without contributing to the development of the revolutionary movement in Europe. The Kremlin's invasion of Czechoslovakia, to take an extreme example, made a big "contribution" to the crisis of Stalinism, although that was far from the intentions of Brezhnev and Co.

The view that Peking should be given credit for contributing "objectively" to the critique of "some of the key features of the bureaucratic rule in Eastern Europe" has not been borne out. It is true that in the early years of the Sino-Soviet dispute (when, as both resolutions agreed, Liu Shao-chi was at the helm in China) the polemics with Moscow were couched in a relatively cautious tone, and the writings of Marx and Lenin were cited to buttress the Chinese case against the Kremlin's offensive. With the advent of the Cultural Revolution Peking escalated its denunciations but did not move toward a Marxist analysis of the dispute.

Mao's thoughts on this question were utilized by the Kremlin to discredit any currents in the Soviet Union sympathetic to Peking. An example was Mao's characterization of the Soviet Union as a "fascist" state in which capitalism had been restored under a "red bourgeoisie." Another example was Peking's adulation of Stalin.

If Mao promoted the struggle for socialist democracy in Eastern Europe by denouncing the "new tsars," shall we say equally that the Kremlin bureaucracy promoted the struggle for socialist democracy in China by denouncing Mao for his "petty-bourgeois policy which became increasingly intertwined with nationalism" and his exercise of "bureaucratic authority"? ("China in the Vice [sic] of Maoism," *Soviet News*, August 5, 1969.)

The logical extension of such reasoning is to be found in Comrade Germain's April 3, 1969, article, "An Unacceptable Amendment." (*Discussion on China*, p. 45.) Here, referring to Peking's opposition to the Soviet invasion of Czechoslovakia in 1968, he wrote:

"In fact, they were fighting on the same side of the barricades as our comrades most of the time, while the Khrushchevists were on the other side."

But Mao is in favor of anything that will weaken his opponents in the Kremlin. If in Czechoslovakia this resulted in Peking ending up on "the same side of the barricades as our comrades," in the Sudan it resulted in Mao applauding the massacre of the CP and trade-union leaders by a bourgeois government because that, too, was a blow to Moscow. Which side of the barricades was Peking on in the Sudan?

It should be remembered that in 1956, before the split with Moscow, Peking supported the crushing of the Hungarian revolution. Its attitude, then as now, was determined by the narrow national interests of the Stalinist bureaucratic caste in China, not by consideration of workers democracy. Moreover, Peking's new-found devotion to the cause of proletarian democracy in the Soviet Union and Eastern Europe does not extend to China, the most obvious test of whether Mao's opposition to bureaucratism stems from revolutionary or opportunist motives. The real reason Mao opposed the Soviet invasion of Czechoslovakia (at the same time, by the way, denouncing the resistance movement as "revisionist") was because the Brezhnev doctrine of "limited sovereignty" established a precedent for Soviet military intervention against China. The clash on the Ussuri river took place less than seven months after the Warsaw Pact occupation of Prague.

II. THEORETICAL ROOTS OF THE DISPUTE IN THE FOURTH INTERNATIONAL

Is Maoism Stalinist or 'bureaucratic centrist'?

On all the principal conjunctural differences on the meaning of the Cultural Revolution and the direction in which Maoism was headed in 1969, the position of the minority of the United Secretariat proved to be correct and the position of the majority proved to be faulty and belied by the later events. But more than conjunctural differences were involved. The underlying appraisals of Maoism by the two sides were and remain sharply divergent. The clearest definition of the nature of Maoism by the leaders of the United Secretariat majority appeared in the article by Comrade Germain cited above ("An Unacceptable Amendment"). There he wrote:

"It has been solid facts that convinced us that on several essential questions, the position of the Chinese remains closer to that of the revolutionary Marxists and more progressive as a whole than that of the Kremlin. . . .

"We do not believe, and we have never said, that the leadership of the Chinese CP is revolutionary. It is a question of a bureaucratic centrist leadership. The fact which we have never ceased to stress is that it is impossible to identify this leadership with that of the Soviet bureaucracy or with Stalinism. It is indispensable to distinguish between them, because this corresponds to the objective reality and because otherwise an effective struggle against Maoism becomes more difficult." (p. 47)

There can of course be no objection to developing in our resolutions and in our press an analysis of the specific characteristics of the Chinese variant of Stalinism as distinct from the Russian variant of Stalinism. These exist and it is necessary to take account of them.

But it is now clear that the differences in the Fourth International on this point do not involve distinguishing the dissimilarities of the two parasitic castes. It has been shown how in the recent past the insistence on the "bureaucratic centrist" character of Maosim led to grave errors as to the aims and intentions of the Peking bureaucracy. The "effective struggle against Maoism" was made more difficult by failing to grasp its Stalinist character, not by failing to distinguish it from the Soviet bureaucracy.

The phrase "bureaucratic centrism" is incorrect in suggesting that the Maoist apparatus and accompanying bureaucratic caste is not yet a fully developed social formation, that it is more responsive to the pressures of the world revolution, and that avenues remain open for the Chinese masses to impress their will on the bureaucratic machine to move it in an "objectively" revolutionary direction.

Comrade Germain insists that it is correct to label Maoism "bureaucratic centrist," to make a qualitative distinction between Maoism and Stalinism, and, moreover, that this has always been the position of the Fourth International. An examination of Trotsky's views and how they were modified by Comrades Maitan, Mandel, and Frank in the resolution they sponsored on the Cultural Revolution should shed some light on this long-disputed question.

The term "bureaucratic centrism" has a very specific meaning in the Trotskyist movement. It originated in reference to the Stalin faction of the CPSU in the 1920s. The Stalin faction then stood in the center between the Left Opposition and the Bukharin right wing of the party. The label was based on the assumption that the Soviet Communist Party remained a working-class party capable of being reformed under the pressure of the masses and the criticism of the Left Opposition. With the consolidation of a bureaucratic caste, the Soviet CP was transformed into a purely administrative agency of the petty-bourgeois bureaucracy, and merged with the state apparatus.

The term "bureaucratic centrism" predated Trotsky's recognition that the Soviet bureaucracy represented a privileged social caste with its own material interests that could be replaced only through political revolution. It was dropped when it became clear that the Soviet Communist Party had been qualitatively changed under Stalin's domination. The term "bureaucratic centrism" to designate Stalinism was then viewed by Trotsky as inconsistent with the call for political revolution.

In 1933 the German CP and the Social Democracy permitted Hitler to take power without a fight. The total default of the Comintern in the face of this historical defeat convinced Trotsky that a new international must be built and that the Stalinist regime had to be ousted through a political revolution. Stalinism had become an opportunist petty-bourgeois current in the world working-class movement.

Trotsky's explicit change in terminology came when he examined in theoretical depth the implications of the term "bureaucratic centrism" in the light of the Left Opposition's new appraisal of the evolution of Stalinism.

In his article "The Workers' State, Thermidor and Bonapartism" (1935) he wrote:

"As the bureaucracy becomes more independent, as more and more power is concentrated in the hands of a single person, the more does *bureaucratic centrism* turn into Bonapartism." (*Writings of Leon Trotsky, 1934–35*, Pathfinder, 1971, 1974, pp. 289–90 [2011 printing]. Emphasis in original.) It was in this same article that Trotsky explained: "The Thermidor of the Great Russian Revolution is not before us but already far behind." (p. 292)

Trotsky concluded: "Stalin guards the conquests of the October Revolution not only against the feudal-bourgeois counterrevolution but also against the claims of the toilers, their impatience and their dissatisfaction; he crushed the left wing that expresses the ordered historical and progressive tendencies of the unprivileged working masses; he creates a new aristocracy by means of an extreme differentiation in wages, privileges, ranks, etc. Leaning for support upon the topmost layer of the new social hierarchy against the lowest—

sometimes vice versa—Stalin has attained the complete concentration of power in his own hands. What else should this regime be called if not Soviet Bonapartism?" (p. 291)

Isn't this a description that applies to the China of Mao as well as to the Russia of Stalin? It is the Bonapartist nature of Stalinism, resting on a "new special hierarchy" and balancing between the working class and world imperialism, that distinguishes it from all varieties of centrist vacillation. To speak of a "right turn" in China without specifying the axis around which the zigzags of the Maoist leadership revolve—the interests of a hardened bureaucratic caste—can lead to illusions as to the underlying determinants of Peking's policies. Such an assessment is suggested by Comrade Maitan in his article on the downfall of Lin Piao written in June 1972. There he writes:

"It would be an error to consider that the positions taken by the Chinese leaders in the most recent period have a definitive character. First of all, the new policy has not yet been sufficiently defined on all levels. Secondly and most importantly, it has always been a characteristic of the Chinese bureaucracy to adapt pliantly to the changes in situations on the basis of an underlying empiricism. In the same way as it shifted gears in 1970–71, it may do so again in the future. For example, if on the international front new dramatic tensions arose in Asia . . . the Chinese leaders might be forced back to a 'hard' line, impelled by the need to stay the hand of imperialism by other means." (*Intercontinental Press*, October 9, 1972, p. 1091.) Maitan adds his estimate that the current opportunist policy of the Peking regime is "likely" to last "for at least a few years."

The notion of a purely empirical (i.e., diplomatic and political) determinant of Peking's line and the hope that Mao will revert to a "hard" line in a few years flow from the view that Maoist Stalinism is an expression of bureaucratic centrism. Trotsky, however, insisted in the late 1930s that such a characterization was inadequate to understand or explain the vacillations of the Stalinist parties. In a letter to James P. Cannon dated October 3, 1937, he wrote:

"Some comrades continue to characterize Stalinism as 'bureaucratic centrism.' This characterization is now totally out of date. On the international arena, Stalinism is no longer centrism, but the crudest form of opportunism and social patriotism. See Spain!" (*Intercontinental Press*, January 22, 1973, p. 57. Also cited in *Writings of Leon Trotsky, 1936–37*, Pathfinder, 1970, 1978, p. 612 [2012 printing].)

Trotsky developed this point further in "Lessons of Spain: The Last Warning" (December 17, 1937). There he wrote:

"The left Socialists and Anarchists, the captives of the Popular Front, tried, it is true, to save whatever could be saved of democracy. But inasmuch as they did not dare to mobilize the masses against the gendarmes of the Popular Front, their efforts at the end were reduced to plaints and wails. The Stalinists were thus in alliance with the extreme right, avowedly bourgeois wing of the Socialist Party. They directed their repressions against the left—the POUM, the Anarchists, the 'left' Socialists—in other words, against the centrist groupings who reflected, even in a most remote degree, the pressure of the revolutionary masses.

"This political fact, very significant in itself, provides at the same time a measure of the degeneration of the Comintern in the last few years. I once defined Stalinism as bureaucratic centrism, and events brought a series of corroborations of the correctness of this definition. But it is obviously obsolete today. The interests of the Bonapartist bureaucracy can no longer be reconciled with centrist hesitation and vacillation. In search of reconciliation with the bourgeoisie, the Stalinist clique is capable of entering into alliance only with the most conservative groupings among the international labor aristocracy. This has acted to fix definitively the counterrevolutionary character of Stalinism on the international arena." (*The Spanish Revolution, 1931–39*, Pathfinder, 1973, p. 382 [2012 printing]. Emphasis in original.)

Thus we see that Trotsky long ago abandoned the term "bureaucratic centrism" for the Soviet bureaucracy and the parties that follow its line. He did not hesitate to use the term Stalinist to designate the Spanish Communist Party, which combined its repression of the centrist POUM and the Trotskyists with leadership of an armed struggle of no small proportions against Franco.

The inherently counterrevolutionary character of Stalinism flows from profound sociological reasons of which its Bonapartist political character is a corresponding reflection. Trotsky, while sharply distinguishing the Soviet bureaucracy from a ruling class, nevertheless noted that it was a far more self-conscious and homogeneous social formation than any previously known bureaucracy. It was for this reason that he labeled it a social caste. In the *Revolution Betrayed*, written in 1936, he said:

"In no other regime has a bureaucracy ever achieved such a degree of independence from the dominating class. In bourgeois society, the bureaucracy represents the interests of a possessing and educated class, which has at its disposal innumerable means of everyday control over its administration of affairs. The Soviet bureaucracy has risen above a class which is hardly emerging from destitution and darkness, and has no tradition of dominion or command. Whereas the fascists, when they find themselves in power, are united with the big bourgeoisie by bonds of common interest, friendship, marriage, etc., the Soviet bureaucracy takes on bourgeois customs without having beside it a national bourgeoisie. In this sense we cannot deny that it is something more than a bureaucracy. It is in the full sense of the word the sole privileged and commanding stratum in the Soviet society." (Pathfinder, 1937, 1972, pp. 257–58 [2009 printing].)

Finally on this point, in his article "The USSR in War," written on September 25, 1939, Trotsky explained his use of the term "caste" to characterize the Soviet regime, distinguishing it from other forms of bureaucracy known in the labor movement in the West or in capitalist state apparatuses. He wrote:

"Our critics have more than once argued that the present Soviet bureaucracy bears very little resemblance to either the bourgeois or labor bureaucracy in capitalist society; that to a far greater degree than fascist bureaucracy it represents a new and much more powerful social formation. This is quite correct and we have never closed our eyes to it. . . . We frequently call the Soviet bureaucracy a caste, underscoring thereby its shut-in character, its arbitrary rule, and the haughtiness of the ruling stratum which considers that its progenitors issued from the divine lips of Brahma whereas the popular masses originated from the grosser portions of his anatomy." (*In Defense of Marxism* [Pathfinder, 1973, 1995], p. 51 [2011 printing])

The Fourth International in all its sections accepted Trotsky's analysis of Stalinism, his call for political revolution against the Soviet bureaucracy, and the identification of pro-Moscow parties, including the Chinese CP, as Stalinist. This remained the position of our movement as a whole until the Chinese revolution of 1949 which posed important theoretical and practical problems for world Trotskyism. In the first tentative estimates of this development made at the Third World Congress in 1951, most of the participants tended to conclude that by the very fact of having taken part in a revolution and having won state power the Maoist CCP had to some degree broken with Stalinism (one exception was Pablo who concluded that the Chinese revolution showed a hitherto unexpected revolutionary potential for parties that remained Stalinist).

The split in the Fourth International in 1954 into two public factions—the International Committee and the International Secretariat—prevented a common world discussion of these important problems. In the period immediately following the split, two distinct views of Maoism emerged in the ranks of world Trotskyism. The Socialist Workers Party in its 1955 resolution on China, drafted for the International Committee in late 1954, concluded that the CCP, despite its having led an armed struggle and despite its rise to state power, remained a Stalinist party that was rapidly consolidating a hardened caste similar in essentials to that in the Soviet Union. This view was shared by Comrade Peng and the Chinese Trotskyists. The resolution stated:

"In terms of political organization the Mao bureaucracy succeeded in the very course of the Third Chinese Revolution in imposing a totalitarian state power. They are now seeking to intrench this bureaucratic superstructure on the proletarian foundation, on the conquests of the revolution. This insolvable contradiction, which characterizes the USSR, and which renders the regime that of permanent crisis, is now being reproduced on Chinese soil, posing before the Chinese workers the iron necessity of political revolution against the bureaucratic caste." ("The Third Chinese Revolution and Its Aftermath," in *The Chinese Revolution and Its Development*, Education for Socialists bulletin, p. 8.)

Comrades Maitan, Mandel, and Frank in 1954 took a position distinct from that of Comrade Peng and the SWP. They held that the CCP's role in the Chinese revolution constituted an objective break with Stalinism and a return to a "bureaucratic centrist" formation of the type represented by the Stalinist faction of the CPSU in the mid-1920s. From this they concluded, consistently if wrongly, that neither a political revolution nor a party of the Fourth International was required in China. This view was expressed in the resolution "The Rise and Decline of Stalinism," adopted by the "Fourth World Congress of the Fourth International" (which was a congress sponsored by the International Secretariat and therefore representative of only a part of the world Trotskyist movement). The resolution stated:

"Since both the Chinese CP and to a certain extent also the Jugoslav CP are in reality bureaucratic centrist parties, which however still find themselves under the pressure of the revolution in their countries, we do not call upon the proletariat of these countries to constitute new revolutionary parties or to prepare a political revolution in these countries. We are working toward the constitution of a left tendency within the JCP and within the Chinese CP, a tendency which will be able, in connection with the development of the world revolutionary rise, to assure and to lead a new stage forward in the revolution in these two countries." (Reprinted in *The Development and Disintegration of World Stalinism,* Education for Socialists bulletin, March 1970, p. 20.)

The resolutions of the Reunification Congress in 1963 make no mention of "bureaucratic centrism" or of any objection to building revolutionary Marxist parties in China or Yugoslavia. The congress outlined a program for workers' democracy in China and stated:

"These conquests cannot be won except through an antibureaucratic struggle on a scale massive enough to bring about a qualitative change in the political form of government." ("The Sino-Soviet Conflict and the Situation in the USSR and the Other Workers' States," Fourth International, October–December 1963, p. 64.)

This formulation stated in essence the need for a political revolution in China, although not explicitly.

It was only at the December 1965 world congress that the concept that the Chinese CP represented a form of centrism was introduced into the documents of the unified International. This took place through amendments and additions to a common resolution on the Sino-Soviet conflict that had been submitted by the world leadership as a whole. These changes were made at a time when Comrade Hansen, who had collaborated on the document for the SWP, was seriously ill and unable to attend the congress. When the alterations in the document came to the attention of the SWP leadership—only after the congress had concluded—they were protested and rejected. (See *The Anatomy of Stalinism,* by Tom Kerry, Education for Socialists bulletin, June 1972, for a discussion of this correspondence.)

The alterations included the introduction of a theory postulating the impossibility of the rise of a bureaucratic caste similar to that in the Soviet Union anywhere else in the world:

". . . the material forces that gave rise to such a hardened and fully crystallized bureaucratic caste as appeared in the Soviet Union no longer exist anywhere in the world." ("The Sino-Soviet Conflict and the Crisis of the International Communist Movement." *International Socialist Review,* Spring 1966, p. 80.)

This uncalled-for assertion was then applied to China:

"The Chinese Communist Party cannot be considered to have been a Stalinist party in the strict sense of the term; that is subordinated since the twenties to the bureaucratic leadership of the Kremlin. The Mao leadership had its own personality; and its policies, although often marked in practice by compromises with the Moscow leadership which led to the gravest deviations, had a generally centrist character leaning toward the left." (Ibid.)

This estimate was carried over in the amendments through which Comrades Maitan, Mandel, and Frank changed the original resolution on the Cultural Revolution in 1969. That document, however, for the first time since the formulation in the 1963 reunification resolution explicitly included a call for political revolution in China. This was a contradictory position. Remnants of the old position of the International Secretariat stood in the way of correctly explaining and anticipating the course of Maoist Stalinism in the recent period.

Maoism as a social formation

The fact is that two different views of Maoism still exist in the Fourth International. This explains why one of the resolutions submitted to the 1969 world congress saw deeper into the character and actions of Maoism than the other. The resolution prepared by Comrades Maitan, Mandel, and Frank, reinforced by Comrade Maitan's report, approached Maoism as a purely *political* phenomenon. Its appraisals were based on study of the programmatic statements and documents issued in Peking.

The original resolution prepared by Comrades Peng, Novack, and Hansen was based on viewing Maoism as a social formation equivalent in essentials to the parasitic caste in the Soviet Union. It was only on this level that a correct understanding of the long-term motivations of the Peking leadership could be reached.

It is true that there is much that is new in the development of Stalinism. Trotsky thought that revolutions in the advanced capitalist countries after World War II would lead to the eclipse and overthrow of Stalinism. But events did not conform to Trotsky's prediction on this score. Stalinism was temporarily strengthened after the war. The developments in Eastern Europe demonstrated that the conditions of caste rule could be duplicated in at least the countries bordering the Soviet Union so long as the Soviet bureaucracy remained in power. We need not repeat here the exceptional circumstances that made this possible.

With the victory of the Chinese revolution in 1949, the Chinese Stalinists found themselves in command of a vast, but extremely poverty-stricken country, which, in the absence of a mass revolutionary Marxist opposition and with help from the Kremlin, favored the growth of a caste on the Soviet model. This process had in fact already begun before 1949 in the remote rural areas where the petty-bourgeois Stalinist leaders exercised command over hundreds of thousands and even millions of peasants through the Maoist "Red Army."

To continue to treat this formation as no more than a bureaucratized political tendency in the workers' movement and not take into account its real social basis as it has become more and more entrenched could only lead to grave mistakes in estimating its inner dynamics and course of development. It is high time for our movement as a whole to apply Trotsky's most important theoretical contribution after the theory of permanent revolution—his analysis of the sociological roots of Stalinism in the material interests of a privileged ruling caste—to the rise of an essentially similar social formation in backward China.

III. A PROGRAM FOR POLITICAL REVOLUTION IN CHINA

A key test of all theories lies in their capacity to correctly forecast events. Our movement from the mid-1930s until the Chinese revolution of 1949 was unanimous in characterizing the Chinese Communist Party as a Stalinist party based on its sociological character and its program. Drawing in a one-sided way on the provisional and on some points erroneous estimates made of the Chinese revolution at the Third World Congress in 1951, a section of the world Trotskyist movement has since 1954 felt that this characterization turned out to be wrong. According to this view, a party that retained a military apparatus and succeeded, under whatever exceptional circumstances, in taking state power could not possibly be Stalinist.

It is almost twenty years since this division of opinion appeared in our ranks. The course of the Cultural Revolution and its aftermath have shown which of these approaches corresponds most closely to the reality.

This should now be recognized by the Fourth International. (1) Maoism should be characterized as a variety of Stalinism and not as "bureaucratic centrism." (2) The general line of the original resolution submitted by the minority of the United Secretariat to the Ninth World Congress should be adopted.

In addition we propose the following as among the main points of a program to establish proletarian democracy in China:

1. The establishment of proletarian democracy is China's most crying need. The will of the toiling majority does not prevail in China today. Instead, a narrow circle of bureaucrats, acting like the crowned heads of an uncontrolled dynasty, decide in secret on all major policies affecting the lives

of hundreds of millions of persons. This state of affairs is fraught with danger for China both at home and abroad.

2. What is immediately required is outlawing of the special privileges of the bureaucracy, the well-spring of the bureaucratic caste. This can be achieved only by structuring the economy and the state on councils controlled by the masses, with the right of all prosocialist tendencies to participate, and with all elected officials subject to immediate recall.

3. This must be accompanied by separation of the party from the state apparatus, abolition of the single-party system, legalization of tendencies within the CCP, and recognition of the right of the masses to assemble and to form opposition parties on the basis of defense of the socialist property forms against attempts from within or without to restore capitalism.

4. To assure proletarian democracy, the masses must have access to accurate information and a wide spectrum of views through a free press, radio, and television.

5. The workers and poor peasants must be guaranteed the right to form unions independent of the state apparatus to enable them to participate without fetters in the elaboration of the economic plan and to safeguard their living standards from encroachment by the state apparatus.

6. National minorities must be granted full national rights, including the right to form independent socialist republics. While representing only 6 percent of the population, the Tibetans, Mongols, Uighurs, Manchus, Chuang, and other minority peoples occupy 60 percent of the land, in the most barren and undeveloped parts of the country.

7. The Mao regime has resisted every tentative effort of the masses to gain proletarian democracy. It is clear that a political revolution is required to overturn the bureaucratic caste and make possible a regime like that of the Paris Commune or of the government headed by Lenin and Trotsky in Russia following the October revolution.

8. The political revolution must be the task of the Chinese workers and poor peasants themselves. They can carry out this task successfully only on condition that the Chinese workers state is defended unconditionally, despite its present leadership, from any attack by imperialism.

The Chinese workers state must likewise be defended against the attempts by the Soviet bureaucracy to impose its will through rattling the nuclear bomb, posting Soviet armies on the Chinese border, and threatening to intervene in the internal affairs of the People's Republic of China.

9. The Chinese Stalinist leaders have demonstrated by their proscription of proletarian democracy, and in the course and outcome of the Cultural Revolution, that it would be delusory to think that the Chinese Communist Party can be reformed. The indispensable instrument for the success of the political revolution is a revolutionary Marxist party, the Chinese section of the Fourth International. The construction of such a party under the difficult conditions imposed by the Mao regime must be the first priority of the class-conscious workers, revolutionary-minded students, and poor peasants in China today.

10. One of the tasks that revolutionists abroad can take up to assist in this process is defense of the political prisoners held by the Maoist regime. Many of these political prisoners, including several score Fourth Internationalists, have been kept imprisoned for more than twenty years. The fate of most of them is unknown. Ways and means must be found to break the wall of secrecy the Chinese Stalinist bureaucracy has maintained over the fate of revolutionists who have dared to speak against the existence of special privileges in a country that is struggling to achieve socialism.

DRAFT RESOLUTION ON THE CULTURAL REVOLUTION IN DUAL COLUMNS

ORIGINAL **PROPOSED AMENDMENTS**

The "cultural revolution" constitutes a momentous dividing line in the political evolution of the People's Republic of China. It marks the irreparable shattering of the nucleus of veteran Communists clustered around Mao, which led the ~~Stalinized~~ Chinese Communist party in the civil war, founded the republic, and overturned capitalist rule, and which, since the victory over Chiang Kai-shek, has run the economy, governed the country, and directed the state and party apparatus. The "cultural revolution" tore this nucleus into contending fragments that cannot be put together.

Initiated in September 1965 by the Maoist faction in the Chinese Communist party leadership, it reached its major objective with the expulsion of Liu Shao-chi from the party at the October 13–31, 1968 "enlarged" twelfth plenum of the Central Committee. Liu, the chief of state, Mao's first lieutenant and main interpreter for several decades, his designated heir until the factional struggle broke into the open, was singled out as the central target of attack under such epithets as "the Khrushchev of China," the "first person in a position of authority who has taken the capitalist road," and, finally, as the "enlarged" twelfth plenum put it, "the renegade, traitor and scab Liu Shao-chi."

Mao has defined the internal struggle which has convulsed China as "in essence a great political revolution under the conditions of socialism made by the proletariat against the bourgeoisie and all other exploiting classes; it is a continuation of the prolonged struggle waged by the Chinese Communist Party and the masses of revolutionary people under its

(delete "Stalinized")

| ORIGINAL | PROPOSED AMENDMENTS |

leadership against the Kuomintang reactionaries, a continuation of the class struggle between the proletariat and the bourgeoisie." (*Peking Review*, No. 43, Oct. 25, 1968.)

This official version bears little resemblance to the truth. The "cultural revolution" is not a "political revolution" for the promotion of workers democracy; it was not made "under the conditions of socialism"; it was not undertaken by the proletariat as the continuation of its struggle against the bourgeoisie. The suggestion that the opposition, which was denied the most elementary rights of proletarian democracy, represented the "Kuomintang reactionaries" is a slander.

The "cultural revolution" represented a phase of sharp public conflict in an interbureaucratic struggle between divergent tendencies in the topmost circles of the Chinese Communist party leadership which eventually affected every sector of Chinese society. It constituted the greatest single crisis experienced by the bureaucratic regime since its ~~establishment~~ establishment and expresses an important weakening of that bureaucratic regime, both as the result of its inner contradictions and of a widespread mobilization of the masses.

2. The sharpness of the innerbureaucratic struggle in China, and the large-scale intervention of the masses in that struggle, can only be understood against the background of objective contradictions and problems which accumulated, since the end of the fifties and the beginning of the sixties, a growing trend of conflicts in Chinese society and a growing discontent among the Chinese masses.

The Chinese People's Republic has registered major accomplishments and made remarkable advances in many fields since the military victory over the Kuomintang in 1949, especially when measured against the relative stagnation of such colonial countries as India, Indonesia and Brazil where capitalism has not been overthrown. ~~However, the authoritarian methods practiced by the Maoist command have grievously hampered solving the colossal problems of economic, social, political and cultural de-~~ However, the colossal problems of economic, social, political and cultural development confronting so backward a country as China, with its huge population, were far from having been solved, and

ORIGINAL

velopment confronting so backward a country as China with its huge population.

The period of intensified difficulties goes back to the damage done to Chinese agriculture and economy during the Great Leap Forward and the 1959–61 near-famine period.

The difficulties at home have been aggravated by the deterioration of Peking's international position due to Mao's foreign policy. This policy, in essence, expresses the narrow national interests of the ruling bureaucracy in China. It has oscillated between opportunism and ultraleftism or combinations of both.

One of the worst setbacks was the break with the Soviet Union. While major responsibility for this lies with the bureaucratic rulers in Moscow, who in the late fifties denied the Chinese government access to nuclear weapons and cut off economic aid, the initiative in extending the rift to the governmental level was taken by Peking.

Moreover, Mao's ultimatism alienated the powerful support and sympathy among the people of other workers states and the ranks of other Communist parties which China had at the beginning of the Sino-Soviet dispute.

Mao's unwillingness or incapacity to promulgate a united front with Moscow served to encourage the expansion of U.S. intervention in Vietnam and a mounting militant danger for China despite the nuclear deterrents which were developed at staggering cost to the Chinese economy.

(delete)

PROPOSED AMENDMENTS

the authoritarian methods practiced by the Maoist leadership have in addition seriously hampered the working out of such solutions.

The main contradictions which the People's Republic of China had to face during the last decade were the following ones:

(a) The contradiction between the rate of growth of the economy, which was still too low, and the rate of growth of the population, which threatened to bring to a near standstill the annual rate of growth per capita real consumption.

(b) The contradiction between the objective necessity to socialize the surplus product of agriculture, for purposes of accelerated economic and industrial development, and the political need to achieve this socialization with the approval of the majority of the peasantry.

(c) The contradiction between the objective necessity to interest materially the bulk of the poor and middle peasantry in increasing agricultural production, and the inevitable tendency to increased inequality and private accumulation which results from these "material incentives."

(d) The contradiction between the general low level of consumption of the mass of the people and the increasing bureaucratic privileges appropriated by the ruling strata in the fifties, and even the early sixties, under conditions of great hardship for the mass of the population.

(e) The contradiction between the objective needs for accelerated industrialization created by the Kremlin's sudden and brutal economic blockade of China.

(f) The contradiction between the rapid expansion of literacy and the increase in general level of education of the Chinese youth at the one hand, and the still relatively low number of skilled jobs available in China.

All these contradictions have been intensified by the damage done to Chinese agriculture and economy during the second phase of the Great Leap Forward and the 1959–61 near-famine period. They created an explosive situation in the country, in which a process of political differentiation and increased political activity of the masses became possible. In this situation, conditions for a genuine

ORIGINAL	PROPOSED AMENDMENTS
	political revolution against the ruling bureaucracy matured. The "cultural revolution" constitutes objectively an attempt by the Mao faction to divert the social forces pushing in that direction from an overthrow of the bureaucracy into a reform of the bureaucracy. 3. Some of the exploding social contradictions accumulated in China during the last decade would have manifested themselves, whatever would have been the inner and outer conditions of the country and the nature of the leadership. Others were greatly sharpened by the autocratic and paternalistic nature of that leadership. All were heavily increased by the sudden isolation into which the People's Republic of China was precipitated in the late fifties, by the Kremlin's sudden suppression of all economic and military assistance to China. This criminal act by the Soviet bureaucracy, extending to state level the factional struggle between that bureaucracy and the Chinese CP inside the world Communist movement, was a stab in the back of the Chinese revolution and the Chinese people, at the very moment when they were confronted with near-famine at home and increased aggressive pressure from U.S. imperialism abroad. It lies at the door of the Kremlin the historic responsibility for breaking up the Sino-Soviet alliance, and the advantages which imperialism could draw from this breakup. The leadership of the Chinese CP, educated in the Stalinist school, has always accepted the theory of "building socialism in one country." However, in the fifties, the importance of the help which the other workers states could give to the economic growth and the military defense of the P.R. of China, made the dangerous implications of that theory inside China less important than in the USSR in the late twenties and the thirties (its international implications detrimental to world revolution continued to manifest themselves even then). The reversal of the Maoist leadership to a policy of "self-reliance" and large-scale economic autarchy and self-sufficiency is only a rationalization of the consequences of the Kremlin's blockade and the tremendous burden imposed on China

| **ORIGINAL** | **PROPOSED AMENDMENTS** |

by the need to develop its own nuclear weapons, given the refusal of the Soviet bureaucracy to assist it on this field.

The more radical line pursued by the Chinese leadership towards world revolutionary developments since the beginning of the Sino-Soviet conflict which, on several important questions, brought it nearer to the positions of revolutionary Marxism (an analysis confirmed in 1968 by Peking's attitude, in contrast to the Kremlin's, towards the May revolution in France, the prerevolutionary struggles in India, the Mexican students' struggles and the rising political revolution in the CSSR leading to the Warsaw Pact countries' occupation of Czechoslovakia), reflects both the specific relationship of imperialism and the Soviet bureaucracy towards the P.R. of China, and the objective impact of the rising tide of world revolution on the Chinese masses.

It is however also true that the bureaucratic character of the Mao faction have added to the international isolation of the P.R. of China and increased the contradictions and political conflicts inside the CP of China.

Although Peking maintained its resolution to defend the USSR against imperialism and the Kremlin failed to reiterate similar assurances to the P.R. of China, Mao failed to promote a consistent policy of anti-imperialist united front in Vietnam, thereby harming the defense of the Vietnamese revolution and the political influence of the CP of China in the world Communist movement.

In place of consistent development of the world revolution, which could have brought new socialist allies into being and carried the struggle for socialism into the main strongholds of the capitalist system, Mao followed a policy of collaborating with the colonial bourgeoisie, as in Pakistan.

[amendment: "a" → "in several countries"]

This helped prepare for the catastrophe in Indonesia, the worst defeat suffered by the world revolution since Stalin permitted Hitler to come to power without a struggle. The development of the cult of Mao, the glorification of Stalin, and opposition to de-Stalinization in the Soviet

ORIGINAL

Union crippled the defense of the Chinese revolution in other lands, reduced Peking's prestige and influence ~~to abysmal levels~~ and gravely injured the cause of socialism internationally.

~~The bankruptcy of this foreign policy became glaringly clear when, after deposing Liu Shao-chi as a "lackey of imperialism, modern revisionism and the Kuomintang reactionaries," Mao offered "peaceful coexistence" to the Nixon administration.~~

The ~~disasters~~ setbacks in foreign affairs heightened the stresses and strains created by the sharpened tensions within Chinese society between the different layers of the peasantry as well as between the peasantry and the state, and between the working class, the student youth, the intellectuals and the bureaucracy in the urban centers. These multiple pressures generated deep differences on domestic and foreign policy in the leadership of the party, government and armed forces. The wisdom of Mao's past decisions and his omniscience came under increasing questioning.

The high officials around Liu apparently sought to close ranks against Mao following the disastrous results of the Great Leap Forward. Liu and his close associates took fright at the appalling consequences of this adventure, counseled retreat, and succeeded in switching over to a more prudent economic course. During this readjustment, the Liu grouping took control of the party apparatus and pushed Mao to one side. Their aim, evidently, was to take ~~this erratic pilot~~ him away from the helm and reduce his status to that of a figurehead while utilizing his prestige to lend maximum authority to their decisions and course of action. Thus they assiduously protected his public reputation for infallibility, a policy that facilitated a comeback for Mao.

By 1965 Mao felt that he was in position to break Liu's hold upon the regime and regain his lost supremacy. By exploiting his immense prestige, by maneuvering between the diverse tendencies and cutting them down one

PROPOSED AMENDMENTS

delete

It can even not be excluded that a change of line of U.S. imperialism towards China would lead to a significant modification of revolutionary militancy advised by the Chinese leadership to its followers abroad—a normalization of relations at state level with the USA being in itself of course not reprehensible.

setbacks

Shift these paragraphs to page 33

him

ORIGINAL

after another, by slandering Liu and his men through a relentless propaganda campaign, Mao succeeded in isolating them and eroding their bases of support among the masses, in the party, the army and the provinces and completing their downfall.

Because of the fragmentary, contradictory and unconfirmed nature of the information available, it is difficult and hazardous to attempt a precise delineation of either the evolution or content of these disagreements. The available evidence indicates that a number of oppositional tendencies were involved. The Maoist machine has not permitted their spokesmen—or they have not dared or cared—to state their positions or platforms publicly, frankly or fully.

The voluminous Maoist polemics, filled with self-contradictions, present obviously falsified accounts and distorted interpretations of the opinions of their opponents and critics. It is, for example, incredible that the head of state Liu Shao-chi, the mayor of Peking Peng Chen and other Political Bureau members such as Teng Hsiao-peng and Tao Chu (the leading Chinese Communists most publicly identified with the Sino-Soviet clashes), the deposed military leaders, the better-known disgraced Communist intellectuals, and other alleged "renegades, enemy agents or counterrevolutionary revisionists" conspired or aspired to bring back capitalism on behalf of "the imperialists and the Kuomintang reactionaries."

Even though the roots, history and specific character of the differences remain obscure and unverified, the consequences of the conflicts they precipitated are clear. The central leading team has been broken up. A period of uncertainty as to the eventual composition and orientation of China's leadership has now opened. Great new forces have been set in motion.

PROPOSED AMENDMENTS

4.

the disagreements inside the leadership of the CP of China.

The high officials around Liu apparently sought to close ranks against Mao following the disastrous results of the Great Leap Forward. Liu and

ORIGINAL	PROPOSED AMENDMENTS
	his close associates took fright at the appalling consequences of this adventure, counseled retreat, and succeeded in switching over to a more prudent economic course. During this readjustment, the Liu grouping took control of the party apparatus and pushed Mao to one side. Their aim, evidently, was to take him away from the helm and reduce his status to that of a figurehead while utilizing his prestige to lend maximum authority to their decisions and course of action. Thus they assiduously protected his public reputation for infallibility, a policy that facilitated a comeback for Mao. By 1965 Mao felt that he was in position to break Liu's hold upon the regime and regain his lost supremacy. By exploiting his immense prestige, by maneuvering between the diverse tendencies and cutting them down one after another, by slandering Liu and his men through a relentless propaganda campaign, Mao succeeded in isolating them and eroding their bases of support among the masses, in the party, the army and the provinces and completing their downfall. The objective basis of this success lies in Mao's capacity to mobilize larger masses, especially of the youth, and to exploit the hatred which had been accumulated in the people against the bureaucracy as a whole. The Liu faction was paralyzed by sticking to the bureaucratic rules and by its inability to question the Mao myth, which it had itself largely contributed to create.
The factional warfare which burst forth in the upper echelons of the bureaucracy passed beyond the confines of the ruling circles in the middle of 1966 after the showdown in the eleventh Central Committee plenum of early August which adopted the 16-point decision on the "cultural revolution." In their maneuvers, they sought support among layers extending far outside the party. A social upheaval was touched off. This unfolded in successive waves, starting with the mustering of the student youth organized from above in the Red Guards, spreading to the industrial workers in the big cities during December 1966–January 1967, stirring up parts of the peasantry, and	5.

seeping into the armed forces.

These interlinked commotions drastically upset the equilibrium of the bureaucratic regime. Despite the present victory of Mao's faction, the turbulent events have weakened its position and power. It will not be able to regain the prestige and stability enjoyed before Mao launched the "Great Proletarian Cultural Revolution." The internecine struggles and the accompanying Maoist propaganda have served to generate new revolutionary energies within the youth and the vanguard elements among the working masses which will not be easily or quickly subdued.

The real situation in China is quite different from the simplistic interpretations offered by various circles. Mao's supporters, and those who take his propaganda at face value, claim that he is promoting an antibureaucratic political revolution against agents of the class enemy, a revolution which aims at and is effectively realizing a wider democracy for the popular masses.

This flies in the face of obvious facts. The authoritarian manner in which the "cultural revolution" was launched, conducted, guided and concluded; the suppression of dissenters, coupled with the conscienceless deformation of the views of the anti-Mao tendencies; the outrageous cult of Mao; the absence of elections and democratic institutions controlled by the workers and peasants; the increased authority of the army under Lin Piao—all testify to the bureaucratic characteristics and direction of the political course taken by the Maoist faction, which has dwindled down to a small core of the old leadership.

Likewise in error are those who view Mao's present position as nothing but a replica of Stalin's tyrannical personal dictatorship. While the bureaucratic ruling castes of the USSR and China have much in common, there are profound differences between the historical situation which enabled Stalin to consolidate his power and the international and domestic

ORIGINAL

context in which Mao advanced the slogan of "seizure of power" by the Red Guards. In China today, the mobilizations of the masses under the impetus of the upheaval, limited ~~and episodic~~ as they have been, have altered the relationship of forces between the bureaucracy and the people to the advantage of the latter. The movement of the masses weakened the bureaucratic regime. This outcome differs from Stalin's rise during the late twenties and early thirties when the masses were crushed and beheaded and fell into a state of unrelieved political passivity which did not appreciably change until after Stalin's death.

The triumph of Mao's faction has by no means eradicated the power of the diversified opposition. Resisters of all sorts remain deeply entrenched in the party, the unions, the army, the universities, the regional committees, the provincial governments the state aparatus, and in the countryside.

As against this, however, the army, under Lin Piao, Mao's new heir apparent and chief lieutenant, has gained greatly in political weight. By virtue of its interventions in the conflicts between the contending bureaucratic factions and between the masses in motion and the regime, the army—at the expense of the leading role of the party—has become the mainstay of Mao's rulership, the chief arbiter and principal centralizing force in the country. This is one of the most dangerous consequences of the "cultural revolution." ~~However much the military high command has been shaken and its leadership divided over the past period, an ominous pattern has been set for the future.~~

6. The "cultural revolution" was prepared and launched ~~by Mao~~ and his liegemen to eliminate the most irritating and ~~persistent~~ critics of his domestic and foreign policy, to give a free hand to his pared-down faction in the top leadership, and, by way of concession to the masses, to curb the worst abuses of the bureaucratic overlords he had himself trained, encouraged and shielded. Having been placed in a minority in

PROPOSED AMENDMENTS

However, Mao tends to reduce again this great weight gained by the army during the previous period, by putting the emphasis on the reconstruction of the party as the mainstay of the regime and the necessity of a single central leadership for all power apparatuses.

ORIGINAL

the Political Bureau, Mao ~~was obliged to take~~ the risk of bypassing the official cadres of the party and state apparatus where his opponents were entrenched, going over their heads, and mobilizing the students of the universities and high schools as the instrument to ~~initiate his coup d'état against the majority leadership.~~

Throughout its course, the Red Guard movement was highly contradictory. Unlike the rebellious student movements in the West, it was initiated from the very summit of state power. It did not have to engage in a "confrontation" with either the police or the armed forces. ~~It operated in collaboration with them or with their blessing. The approbation of the country's living deity helped direct the energies of the Red Guard movement along the course selected for it, so that even in its rebellion against the bureaucratic authority it did not transcend the broad limitations set by the supreme bureaucrat.~~

~~The tendency of the Red Guards toward conformism could be observed at first hand in the West when the Chinese students studying abroad were recalled (not to be replaced to this day). Some of these unfortunates went to extraordinary lengths to arrive home as bandaged heroes, victims of either the Western police or the Khrushchevist bureaucracy.~~

~~The excursions of roaming bands of youth, numbering in the millions, were fostered and financed by the state, either directly or indirectly. Besides facilitating the development of the Red Guard movement in this way, Mao used even stronger means to force its pace of growth. The schools were shut down by decree, China's entire educational system being dealt a blow of immense proportions, the effects of which will be felt for a long time to come.~~

The fact that the Red Guard movement was initiated from above and not by the youth themselves greatly facilitated the efforts of other sectors of the bureaucracy to counter Mao's factional action by setting up Red Guard groups under their own auspices. Since all the

PROPOSED AMENDMENTS

took

reestablish his control over the country.

except in its initial stage.

delete

ORIGINAL	PROPOSED AMENDMENTS
groups were formed under the guise of carrying out Mao's directives and Mao's "thought," ~~the confusion was immense.~~ Nevertheless many of the groups became differentiated sufficiently in their interpretations of Mao's doctrines to come to blows and worse.	Mao's "thought," it was difficult for broader masses to understand their political differences.
Where civil strife reached proportions bordering on civil war, whether through ~~excesses of~~ the Red Guards or through their incapacity to actually "seize power" for Mao in areas where opposing forces were strongly entrenched, the army moved in. Thus behind the Red Guard movement stood the army as the final authority, sometimes ~~instigating~~ the bands of youth, at other times restraining them or even reversing what they had done.	differences among

manipulating |

It would be a mistake, nonetheless, to view the Red Guard movement as merely a pliant instrument of factional politics in the domestic strife that featured the "cultural revolution." The Chinese student youth had many grievances comparable to those of youth in other lands today. These included social discrimination in the selection of the student body, inadequate living quarters, lack of campus autonomy, and scant opportunities after graduation. They resented haughty and uncontrolled bureaucratic authority; they wanted greater democracy; they wanted a political revolution to open the road to socialist democracy; they identified their fate with that of the world revolution.

This explains why Mao had such difficulty retaining control of the Red Guard movement and curbing it once it had served the main purposes he envisioned. The Red Guard movement acquired a logic of its own.

Roaming the countryside on their own, engaging in actions of a violent nature against echelons of the bureaucracy, millions of youth gained in self-confidence and boldness. The most unmanageable of these elements passed beyond the specific objectives set for them by their bureaucratic patrons and even collided with them. Their tendency to move in the direction of critical thought and independent political action was observable in many of the wall posters and mimeographed or printed publications put out by the Red Guards and in some of the "seizures of power" in which they engaged. The movement became so dangerous to Mao's objectives that he finally found it advisable to demobilize the Red Guards and send them back to the classrooms or the countryside for labor.

However, ferment persists among them. The most advanced and revolutionary-minded members of this new generation, who received their political baptism in the "cultural revolution," may later detonate further mass actions against the Chinese bureaucracy as a whole, including the Maoist victors.

Of greater significance than the Red Guard demonstrations was their sequel when the proletarian masses were drawn into the expanding struggle from December 1966 through February 1967. Taking advantage of the splits among the contending factions on top and spurred into action by one or another of them, sectors of the work force began to put forward their own economic and social demands and move along independent lines. This action flared into general strikes in transportation and many plants in Shanghai, Nanking, and other industrial centers.

The movement from below, which in its further development would have threatened the control of the Maoist leadership, was stopped short by combined methods of manipulation and repression. The brevity of the massive strikes does not diminish their historic import. They signaled the end of political apathy among the industrial workers and the resumption of their autonomous action.

~~The Maoist press depicts the "cultural revolution" as a clear-cut class conflict between staunch defenders of socialism and the proletariat under "the wise leadership of our great leader Chairman Mao," and "a bunch of counterrevolutionary revisionists" and "repre-~~ *(delete)*

ORIGINAL

sentatives of the bourgeoisie who have sneaked into the Party, the government, the army and various spheres of culture" in order, when conditions are ripe, to "seize political power and turn the dictatorship of the proletariat into a dictatorship of the bourgeoisie."

Actually, an assortment of political currents holding different views and oriented in various directions have emerged from the disintegration of the formally monolithic bureaucracy and the turmoil of the "cultural revolution." Some of the features of these currents are distinguishable despite the concern of all of them to wear the same uniform of "Mao's Thought."

The two principal groupings vying for supremacy in the party, state apparatus and the army centered around Mao Tse-tung and Liu Shao-chi. On the fringes of these two groupings stand oppositional tendencies of rightist or leftist coloration.

Neither of the chief factions contending for supremacy within the Chinese Communist bureaucracy is striving for socialist democracy or has a program of revolutionary policies at home and abroad. By Marxist standards, neither of the chief factions deserves political support against its rival. From the available information—and it is admittedly scanty and inadequate —neither faction can be judged to be more progressive than the other.

As long as Liu's group retained supremacy it practiced the abominable customs of bureaucratic command learned in the school of Stalinism. Its doctrines and practices were indistinguishable from those of the previous period when Mao was in direct control. The pent-up hatred among the youth, the workers and peasants enabled Mao to arouse these forces against the bureaucratic majority without much trouble.

While the Mao faction has issued calls for rebellion and appeals to the initiative of the masses, its deeds do not harmonize with its words. Mao's objective was to regain suprem-

PROPOSED AMENDMENTS

[delete the bracketed paragraph beginning "Actually, an assortment..."]

7.

insert "actually" before "striving"; insert "genuine" before "revolutionary"

ORIGINAL

acy for his faction and line in the bureaucracy, not overthrow the bureaucracy. This explains why he followed the Stalinist methods of slander, physical violence and the fostering of cultism in his struggle and strictly limited his appeals to the masses. Whenever and wherever any segment of the people, whether among the youth, the proletariat, the peasantry or the intellectuals, has showed signs of slipping away from domination and direction by Mao to act on its own account, it has been restrained and called to order, sometimes by repressive measures.

The promise held out in section 9 of the original 16-point program in the official declaration of the "cultural revolution," adopted by the August 1966 Central Committee plenum, of "a system of general elections, like that of the Paris Commune," which would usher in an extensive democracy, sounds like a mockery today. Not only have no ~~free general~~ **such** elections been held, but the very idea is now scoffed at ("Blind faith in elections is also a form of conservative thinking.")

Instead of instituting an expanded workers democracy on the model of the Paris Commune, Mao has reorganized the bureaucrat-regime under the auspices of "the triple alliance," regulated by the army and presided over by that part of the cadres loyal to his faction. The "revolutionary committees" set up during the "cultural revolution" have not been elected by the working masses themselves and kept under their surveillance by measures of democratic control but have been constituted ~~of individuals handpicked by the authorities.~~ **by compromise between contending factions under the supervision of the Mao–Lin Piao hard core.**

There have been reports of elements on the left flanks of the contending top factions, both among Mao's followers and among the workers and intellectuals sympathetic to Liu and other disgraced leaders, who have revolutionary ideas and inclinations and who could form the nuclei of a genuinely antibureaucratic opposition. These revolutionists deserve international support. However, under current conditions,

ORIGINAL

it is extremely difficult for such dispersed left Communists to come together, to communicate with one another, to work out a common program, select leaders, and undertake a consistent line of organized activity.

The most ironic aspect of the vaunted Great Proletarian Cultural Revolution is the damage it has inflicted upon the cultural life of China. The witch-hunt and persecution of intellectuals, the stifling of discussion and the bridling of free inquiry; the closing down of the universities and high schools for almost two years; the demand that all fields of creative and artistic endeavor submit to the arbitrary specifications laid down by state and party authorities; the universal chanting of obligatory phrases to Mao Tse-tung in the style of a primitive religion creates an atmosphere completely inimical to the development of a humanistic culture permeated with the ideals and critical thought of socialist liberation. Cultural creativity and activity must wither under conformism and regimentation of thought where the expression of dissenting views on all issues of concern to the nation are tabooed and penalized.

The grotesque cult of Mao, who has been elevated like Stalin before him to the height of a semicelestial being with powers bordering on the supernatural, is utterly antipathetic to the critical spirit of Marxism and the development of a socialist culture. Some 3.4 billion sets of Chairman Mao's writings and reproductions of his portrait have been issued during the "cultural revolution" and his name is invoked about five million times a day on the air. Ludicrous and repulsive as this is after the lessons of the adulation accorded to Stalin, the deification of Mao serves a practical political function. The reverence for Mao among the masses, serving as an opiate of the people, is an indispensable source of stability for the Chinese bureaucracy. His disappearance from the scene will precipitate a problem of succession more perilous for the present regime than was the death of Stalin for the Soviet bureaucracy.

PROPOSED AMENDMENTS

delete

ORIGINAL	PROPOSED AMENDMENTS
The Maoists accuse their adversaries of "revisionism." But the very arguments they invoke to justify their current course show that they are ~~even more guilty than~~ their opponents of blatantly revising a number of the basic tenets of Marxism.	8. as guilty as

(1) In countries that have overthrown the bourgeoisie and abolished private ownership of the means of production, they assert that capitalism can be restored by gradual and peaceful processes through machinations and false policies of one or another tendency in the leadership of the Communist parties. This discards or disregards the Marxist theory of the state which asserts that such fundamental changes cannot be accomplished either gradually or peacefully.

(2) They identify the bureaucratic degeneration of the revolution with capitalist restoration. In doing this, the Maoists lapse into an extreme voluntarism, enormously exaggerating the social weight of ideology. Mao locates the chief cause of the danger of bureaucratic degeneration and capitalist restoration, not in the material foundations of the socio-economic order, but in the realm of ideology. He proclaims that if revisionism is not rooted out on the theoretical, scientific, artistic and literary levels, it will inevitably lead to the overthrow of the dictatorship of the proletariat.

Marxists have never believed that the *ideas* of those reactionary classes which have lost economic and political power as the result of a social revolution are capable of gradually changing the class nature and structure of the state. A colossal counterrevolution of this kind could occur only through a civil war between the former possessing classes and the toiling masses in which the masses were crushed; or through the hypothetical generation of a new bourgeoisie which became strong enough economically to launch a civil war and topple the workers state. This has not happened, and it is far from happening, not only in China but in other workers states whose leaderships are

ORIGINAL	PROPOSED AMENDMENTS

at odds with Peking, whatever the incipient tendencies may be in these countries in the direction of capitalism.

(3) No less voluntaristic is the Maoist belief that incessant appeals to the spirit of sacrifice, the idealism and enthusiasm of the toiling masses can in and of themselves suffice to surmount the immensely difficult problems arising from the inadequate development of the productive forces in China during the transition from capitalism to socialism.

(4) In defiance of the historical lessons drawn by Lenin in *State and Revolution*, the Maoists proclaim that in the period of transition from capitalism to socialism the class struggle is bound to intensify and not diminish, and can even go on for hundreds of years. This "theory" serves to justify intensifications of the role of the state as a repressive instrument. The state, instead of withering away under socialism as Engels forecast, will endure for an indefinite period, if Mao is correct. Thus a "theoretical" excuse is provided for the worst bureaucratic excesses and abuses of power.

(5) The strategy of world revolution expounded by Mao and Lin Piao extols the insurrectionary movements of the peasantry in the backward colonial areas and systematically underrates or dismisses the key role which the industrial working class in the advanced countries must play in overthrowing the power of imperialism and helping to create the new socialist society.

The "cultural revolution" has given widespread currency to the idea that a workers state can become subjected to deformation and degeneration after the conquest of power, an idea that was previously propagated only by the world Trotskyist movement. Coming after the antibureaucratic campaigns in Yugoslavia and Cuba, the Maoist propaganda on this point, distorted though it is, has focused attention upon one of the most crucial problems confronting a victorious socialist revolution: how to protect and promote workers democracy.

9.

ORIGINAL

The need for a political revolution where state power has been usurped by a bureaucracy and all avenues of democratic control have been closed to the masses has been made clearer and more understandable to broad sections of the international Communist movement and the revolutionary vanguard. This lesson has been reinforced by the abrupt and brutal halting of the drive toward democratization in Czechoslovakia in 1968 by the Soviet occupation.

If the "cultural revolution" has helped popularize and win acceptance of the notion of political revolution in the bureaucratized workers states, its course and outcome under the tutelage of Mao Tse-tung demonstrates that the methods pursued by his faction leads to the opposite result. It is impossible to eradicate bureaucracy by bureaucratic means. ~~The "cultural revolution" has ended in the constriction of democracy and the fortification of the positions of one faction of the bureaucracy against its rivals rather than the expansion and deepening of decision-making powers by the masses.~~

There is no other road for effective struggle against the bureaucatic degeneration of the revolution and the authoritarian regimes it spawns than the program outlined by Lenin and Trotsky; that is, the consolidation and institutionalization of workers power on the basis of democratically elected councils, the widest proletarian democracy, the right of various socialist tendencies and parties to exist legally within that constitutional framework, the limitation and progressive abolition of inequality in remuneration, the management of the economy by the workers themselves, the planned development of the productive forces, and the international exten-

PROPOSED AMENDMENTS

(delete)

The "cultural revolution" has ended in an attempt to stop the mass movement and to restore a new form of bureaucatic rule, under the guise of the "triple alliance," instead of the rule of the old party and state bureaucracy which had, in its majority, supported Liu. This "triple alliance" is in reality a compromise between the Maoist faction and parts of the old majority faction, compromise initiated when the masses started to intervene autonomously into the struggle and thereby threatened the whole bureaucratic rule.

ORIGINAL

sion of the revolution, above all, to the centers of imperialism.

❧

The position of the Fourth International on the Chinese revolution, which has been set forth in numerous documents and declarations in recent years, can be summarized as follows:

The Fourth International has been a firm supporter of the socialist revolution in China from its beginning. Its partisans within China and throughout the world stand for the unconditional defense of the People's Republic of China against military attack by U.S. imperialism or any of its vassal states.

The Fourth International holds the Kremlin leadership primarily responsible for the Sino-Soviet split, condemns its vengeful withdrawal of economic aid from China, and its continued diplomatic deals with Washington, Paris, New Delhi and other bourgeois governments against the People's Republic of China.

At the same time, the Fourth International criticizes the ultrasectarian attitude and bitter-end factionalism exhibited by Peking in its relations with other workers states that do not fully endorse its policies. Especially harmful has been its stubborn refusal to propose or participate in joint action with the Soviet Union, Cuba and other Communist countries against U.S. intervention in Vietnam because of political disagreements with them.

While recognizing that for its own reasons Peking often pursues a more aggressive diplomatic policy than Moscow, the Fourth International also criticizes the opportunism of the Chinese Communist leadership. In seeking to gain influence in the colonial world, Peking uses a language that is strongly anti-imperialist. It has extended material aid to guerrilla forces as well as countries like Tanzania, thus helping to create an image far to the left of Moscow. Nevertheless, Peking's basic policy, as reiterated many times by its leaders and voiced

PROPOSED AMENDMENTS

10.

them, although some practical agreements on military assistance to Vietnam were finally concluded.

advocates a more militant line to its followers abroad

bureaucratic centrism

delete

It has extended material aid to guerrilla forces. This has not only created an image far to the left of Moscow but also objectively favored anti-imperialist struggles in various parts of the world, especially Southeast Asia, the Arab countries and

ORIGINAL

~~once again upon the inauguration of the Nixon administration, has been "peaceful coexistence" with U.S. imperialism. Out of narrow nationalistic considerations and in line with its doctrine that the revolution must first pass through a bourgeois stage before it can reach the socialist stage, Peking counsels and countenances support to bourgeois governments in Indonesia, Pakistan and other countries instead of mobilizing the masses for uncompromising struggle against the neocolonial regimes.~~ *(delete)*

The conduct of the Chinese Communist party leadership since it came to power proves that it has not shaken off its Stalinist heritage. These ~~nationalistic-minded~~ *(delete)* bureaucrats do not hesitate to subordinate the welfare of the Chinese masses and the interests of the international revolution and socialism to the protection and promotion of their own power and privileges.

The same features mark the policies and behavior of the Maoist groups that have appeared in numerous countries since the Sino-Soviet split. They mix adventurism with opportunism. They have shown themselves incapable of critical or independent thought along Marxist lines. As a result, most of them display little internal cohesion and tend generally to splinter into warring fragments.

~~In a few areas newly radicalized youth have mistaken the verbal militancy and activism of the Maoist groups as representing Marxist-Leninism in contrast to the cowardly reformism of the Social Democrats and the opportunism of Moscow and its followers. With experience this initial impression soon fades in~~ *(delete)*

PROPOSED AMENDMENTS

Africa. Likewise, the sharp campaign which Peking unleashed against the right-wing opportunist line of the CP's following Moscow's lead, and against some key features of the bureaucratic rule in Eastern Europe, has objectively contributed to deepen the world crisis of Stalinism and to facilitate the upsurge of a new youth vanguard the world over. Inside that youth vanguard the general sympathy for China and Maoist criticism of the Kremlin's revisionism remains deep, even if extreme organizational sectarianism and political infantilism has prevented the orthodox Maoists from stabilizing important youth organizations anywhere.

On the other hand, Peking's basic policy has continued to imply support to whatever bourgeois government in a semicolonial country happens to diplomatically collaborate with China (yesterday Indonesia, today Pakistan and Tanzania), which leads to disastrous results for the revolutionary class struggle in these countries.

| ORIGINAL | PROPOSED AMENDMENTS |

~~most instances. Almost ten years after the Sino-Soviet dispute began, the Maoists have still proved incapable of creating a sizeable youth movement in any country outside of China or providing substantial or lasting programmatic inspiration to the leaderships of the new generation of rebel youth advancing into the political arena on an international scale.~~ — delete

The experience of the "cultural revolution" offers fresh evidence that ~~the crystallized bureaucratic caste headed by Mao cannot be reformed~~ — also in China, the bureaucracy cannot be removed by reforms. It will have to be removed from power by the new vanguard of genuine revolutionaries now in the process of formation in China who will come to the head of the aroused and organized masses in the subsequent development of an authentic antibureaucratic revolution. Such a resurgent independent movement will break the grip of the bureaucracy over China's economic, political and cultural life and really expand and consolidate the workers democracy which the "cultural revolution" promised in its propaganda but lamentably failed to deliver.

THE DIFFERENCES BETWEEN THE TWO DOCUMENTS ON THE 'CULTURAL REVOLUTION'

By Joseph Hansen

Based on a report and discussion at two meetings of the New York branch of the Socialist Workers Party June 11 and June 18.

I assume that all of you have read the two resolutions published in issue No. 5 of the *International Information Bulletin* and that you may have had some difficulty in determining the meaning of the differences to be found between them.

We had the same problem in the national leadership when we received the suggested list of amendments to the original draft. To facilitate the analysis, we prepared a document with the original resolution running in one column and the suggested amendments in a parallel column. By following this, it was easier for us to see what was involved. It appeared to us that the amendments were of considerable scope, really representing two divergent approaches, and that it would be in the interests of clarification to stand on the original document without making any changes. It would thus be easier to follow the discussion from its very origin.

We intended to distribute the document presenting these dual columns at the world congress. Unfortunately the bundle was forgotten, and that's why we have a number of copies here so that you will be able to follow the columns in the discussion this evening.

Comrade Livio Maitan gave a report on the "Cultural Revolution" on behalf of the majority of the United Secretariat. This will be published in a forthcoming issue of *Intercontinental Press*, and you will be able to read it and study it there for yourself at your leisure. To forestall any expectations, I should like to mention that Comrade Livio in his report does not deal directly at all with the differences appearing in the two resolutions. This was somewhat of a handicap to clarifying these differences at the world congress.

There were two opposition reports. One was given by Comrade Ross Dowson on behalf of the minority of the United Secretariat. This is the position represented by the resolution in the left-hand column, called "original" in the document which you have before you.

The other opposition report was given by Comrade Peng, who, as you know, was one of the founders of the Chinese Communist movement. Briefly, Comrade Peng took the position that critical support should have been given to the Liu Shao-chi faction. He was against abstaining in the factional conflict in China. Comrade Peng's report is not yet available. However, his position can easily be studied, having been presented in previous bulletins.

As I mentioned, the two resolutions on which the congress had to decide may appear at first glance to be almost the same. Therefore, to many delegates it seemed rather strange that these two resolutions should be presented as opposing resolutions. Yet the main interest at the congress when this point came up on the agenda centered around the differences between them.

I don't want anyone to think that we regard the original text as something sacred. It has never been our tradition to elevate any text into something untouchable. And I would say that the comrades of the majority rather took the same attitude toward their version after they had finished working on it. In their view, I imagine, it still remained unsatisfactory. This is indicated by the nature of the report which Comrade Livio Maitan gave, which appeared to me to be intended to fill in the gaps as they saw them and to strengthen the resolution from their point of view.

In considering the resolution—the original, that is—it is quite essential to understand its purpose. This was conceived as being, first of all, an assessment of the "Cultural Revolution" in China as an event that had occurred since the previous congress—no more than that; simply assess the "Cultural Revolution" without taking up the much broader question of the Chinese revolution as a whole. In addition to that, the purpose of the resolution was to set a political line in relation to the "Cultural Revolution," to the factions involved in the struggle in the "Cultural Revolution," and to set a political line in relation to the Maoist tendency internationally.

We began with the assumption that it had been recognized by our movement that a hardened bureaucratic caste and a corresponding regime exist in China and that the "Cultural Revolution" provided incontrovertible evidence of the accuracy of this estimate.

The "Cultural Revolution" did not lead to any greater proletarian democracy in China. It did not lead to any greater control by the masses of the regime in China. And the main strategic objective in the resolution as we prepared it was a political revolution. In the process of advancing this aim, our position was that it was inadvisable to support either the Mao faction or the Liu Shao-chi faction.

Thus, the resolution was intended to serve a rather narrow function, that is, to make a political delineation between Trotskyism and Maoism.

The sharpness of tone in the resolution was intended for a specific purpose. That is, to set a general attitude, a general political way of looking at the Maoists and their position. It was not intended to be a balance sheet of the Chinese revolution, a much more ambitious project. It did not attempt to probe the origins of the "Cultural Revolution" in detail, because in our opinion there is not yet sufficient factual material to enable us to do that satisfactorily. There are very few documents available in China or abroad presenting accurate, detailed information on the positions of the different contending forces, what their origin was, and how they developed.

And the original resolution did not attempt to forecast the ultimate consequences of the "Cultural Revolution." That's rather difficult, and rather hazardous in the absence of sufficient material to determine the exact origin and development and relationship of forces in China.

In short, the original resolution was intended to be strictly conjunctural. It was intended simply to provide a guiding line for the immediate period ahead, following the congress and up to the next congress, which should be held within two years or so.

The original resolution was tied in with what we conceive to be the main task of the international Trotskyist movement in the immediate period ahead, that is, to win leadership among the radicalizing youth, where we find ourselves faced with the challenge of Maoism, which we have to meet in any number of ways, in different areas, including inside the U.S., as you well know. These were the considerations that determined in our thinking the character and limits of the resolution.

At the congress, we discovered that these limitations, which were deliberate ones, met with a good deal of criticism. Various delegates considered this not to be a high-level document. By "high level," they mean a document that covers a wide field, offers an abundance of material, and generally includes a liberal number of footnotes to show that the available printed material in the field has been consulted.

So evidently there were two concepts at the congress of what a resolution of this nature should seek to accomplish. Some comrades seemed to be of the opinion that the best type of resolution is a "flood" document. We preferred one stripped down to the essence of the question, making it easier to single out those aspects on which one may have a disagreement. The bulky side, in our opinion, is best supplied in signed articles, or statements of an article type, which can be published in conjunction with current events.

So now with these preliminary remarks, what I want to do is take the two documents as presented in the two columns and indicate why we reached certain opinions and conclusions concerning the changes that were made in the original.

The first one, in the first column, is simply one word. The word "Stalinized" has been deleted from the phrase "Stalinized Chinese Communist party."

When I first saw that deletion, I did not immediately hit the ceiling. From an editorial viewpoint, we very often have to take out adjectives, and we're not too concerned about that, because we don't hold adjectives to be sacrosanct. It was only later, as we proceeded studying the changes, that we began to think that possibly there were other reasons than editorial ones for removing this particular word. My first reaction, as I said, was that the comrades thought it might be misunderstood; maybe it could be regarded as an epithet.

But then the question arises, who will object to such an epithet? Why should the leaders of the Chinese CP object to their party being called "Stalinized," when they're very proud of Stalin and their association with him, display portraits of Stalin, hold him almost in equal reverence with Mao himself, and are utterly opposed to de-Stalinization? From their viewpoint, the world "Stalinized" might be taken as a compliment.

Actually, the only people who could really feel uncomfortable about our using the word "Stalinized" in connection with the Chinese Communist party are those who want to support Mao, but who do not want to support him in a package deal that includes Stalin. They're the ones who object to it.

At the congress, this type of objection was not raised very seriously, because it was very hard to maintain that the Maoists would take offense at being called Stalinists, a label they consider to be very apropos.

Several delegates did raise the objection that if we used the word in this particular place it would indicate a certain concept of the Chinese Communist party when it took power—that it was Stalinized then. This would then create a great theoretical difficulty, it was maintained, because how can a Stalinized party take power?

It would have been interesting to have had a discussion on this point at the congress, but this did not occur. And so I can only raise certain questions in the light of what was intimated on this point at the congress.

For instance, if you say that the Chinese Communist party was not Stalinized then the opposite conclusion can be drawn, the conclusion that you must say it was revolutionary, since only a revolutionary party can take power. We had some discussion on this question in the SWP, and you will recall that this was essentially the position taken by Arne Swabeck. He eventually came to the position that the Chinese CP could not have come to power unless it was revolutionary. Since it did come to power, it was therefore revolutionary.

The question nevertheless arises, when did it become revolutionary? We know that at one point it was not revolutionary; it was Stalinist. At what point did it change? This is a very crucial question from the viewpoint of theory.

Other questions arise. What was the evidence of this change? What was the point of qualitative change? Answering these doesn't get us out of the woods either, because the same questions must be asked concerning the regime today. Is the regime today a Stalinized regime? If it is not a Stalinized regime, then why should we call for a political revolution?

If it is a Stalinized regime, but was previously revolutionary, when did it become Stalinized? If you hold that the CP was not Stalinist when it took power, but is Stalinist today, the question must be answered, when did it change from being not Stalinist to being Stalinist? What was the point of qualitative change? You have to determine that to adequately complete our theoretical appreciation of the Chinese revolution.

There's still another possibility that can be suggested. That is, you can eliminate the label "Stalinized" or "Stalinism" altogether in reference to the Mao regime. Just not use such words. There are various ways this can be plausibly done.

You can do it, for instance, by saying that Stalinism only applies to the Soviet Union. The difficulty with that is that Stalinism is an international phenomenon—a well-known international phenomenon.

Or you can take another tack; you can say that Stalinism existed only for a period in the Soviet Union, the period of the purges, the period say from 1934 to 1937. If you do that, then, of course, it is easy to come to the conclusion that the label "Stalinism" is not applicable to China. You can't apply the term Stalinism to China, if it's only applicable to the Soviet Union in the period 1934–37.

But then we run into another problem—what about the reverence with which Stalin is regarded by the Maoists? How do you explain that? Still more important, what about the business of carrying on Stalinist practices? Of imitating the Stalinist pattern of rule? Of fostering special privileges, however modest the scale, in the Stalinist tradition?

Moreover, if you are to be consistent, then you should say that in the Soviet Union Stalinism ceased to exist after about 1937. It ceased to exist during Stalin's lifetime.

That would confront us with a major problem—how to explain on the level of theory the continuity of bureaucratic rule in the Soviet Union from that period up to the present time. Not to mention the question of "de-Stalinization."

So you see that if we try to simply eliminate this designation, we create a lot more problems than we evade.

My opinion is that we ought to retain the label, and try to find some other solution.

So much for the first change in the original document.

At the bottom of the same page—page 1—a phrase has been added. The phrase refers to the weakening of the regime owing to its inner contradictions and the mobilization of the masses during the "Cultural Revolution." We have no objection to the statement being included here. The point is made later in the resolution, so it could be argued that it is superfluous to add it here.

On page 2, we come to a rather considerable substitution. The first paragraph of the substitution, which begins with the number 2, is merely introductory. Further down is a list of contradictions, beginning with "a" and ending with "f."

Comrade Livio Maitan's report was devoted almost wholly to proving that these contradictions are real and do exist in China. He cited considerable evidence with regard to this. Now we have no objection to that; as a matter of fact, I think there is nothing wrong in making a list of contradictions like this. In studying the Chinese revolution as a whole, it is necessary to begin with such a list. But the question remains to be answered: How do they relate to the "Cultural Revolution?"

Comrade Peng made the point, for example, that contradiction "a"—which deals with the rate of growth of the population in relation to the rate of growth of the economy—has been true of China for the past 100 years and is also true of some other countries. To include this contradiction in a list offers little to enable us to better understand the specific phenomenon of the "Cultural Revolution." Comrade Peng made a telling criticism, I think.

His criticism is even substantiated by the statement made by the comrades of the majority on page 3 in the paragraph beginning with the number 3: "Some of the exploding social contradictions accumulated in China during the last decade would have manifested themselves, whatever would have been the inner and outer conditions of the country and the nature of the leadership."

If this statement is correct—and I think that it must be granted that it is correct—then at least some of the contradictions listed would not enable us to distinguish between developments under the Mao regime and under a regime headed by a Lenin or Trotsky. No matter what the "nature of the leadership," we are told, some of the contradictions listed would have confronted the country. For the sake of clarity, it would have been well if the comrades of the majority had indicated which ones.

Further, on this same point. If some of the contradictions listed by the majority would have "manifested themselves" no matter what the nature of the leadership, they offer no means for making a precise analysis of the "Cultural Revolution," for it follows that the "Cultural Revolution" could have occurred just as well under a Trotsky as under a Mao.

The contradictions listed are, in fact, so general that the comrades of the majority felt compelled to say that they would have manifested themselves no matter what China's general situation might have been both domestically and internationally.

It must be admitted that Comrade Peng put his finger on a considerable weakness in the majority's list of contradictions when he called attention to their extremely abstract nature.

And when you read Comrade Maitan's report, which will soon appear in *Intercontinental Press* as part of the documents of the world congress, you will be able to see for yourself that with regard to the crucial question of precisely how these general contradictions came to be specifically expressed in the "Cultural Revolution," he has nothing to say. There is a gap in his report precisely where concreteness is demanded.

To fill that gap it is necessary to consider at least five more contradictions which were apparently overlooked by the comrades of the majority.

Let me list them:

1. The contradiction between the narrow national interests of the bureaucracy and the international interests of the Chinese revolution.

Understanding this contradiction is basic to understanding the foreign policy followed by Mao and the possible criticisms of it in China from various quarters that may have helped precipitate the intense factional dispute which Mao called the "Cultural Revolution."

2. The contradiction between the objective national need to overhaul policies and leaders from top to bottom, that is, to break up the bureaucratic crust, and the need felt by this social layer to retain its position, its power, and its special privileges.

Understanding this contradiction is basic to understanding the specific disputes in the "Cultural Revolution," whether they involved the masses against the bureaucracy as a whole, or sectors of the bureaucracy in dispute with each other, or combinations of these.

3. The contradiction between the professed aims of the Great Leap Forward and its actual catastrophic results.

Understanding this contradiction is basic to understanding the references among the contending forces in the "Cultural Revolution" to the period of the Great Leap Forward. In the minds of all the politically conscious layers in China, the Great Leap Forward remains the outstanding example of the ill-advised and costly ventures which the regime is capable of plunging the entire country into.

4. The contradiction between the need for a thoroughgoing criticism of the Great Leap Forward and Mao's need to foster, maintain, and expand the cult of his personality and Thought.

Understanding this contradiction is basic to understanding the obscure disputes, formation of cliques, tendencies, and undeclared factions that culminated in the "Cultural Revolution."

5. The contradiction between the need for de-Stalinization and Mao's need to maintain the prestige of having been right in hailing and following Stalin and in reproducing in China the Stalinist pattern of rule.

Understanding this contradiction is basic to understanding why the "Cultural Revolution" ended in the monstrous growth of the Mao cult instead of the establishment of any institutions of proletarian democracy let alone elections on the model of the Paris Commune as promised by Mao at the beginning.

No doubt other contradictions of a similar nature could be added, but these should be sufficient to indicate the point.

If it were possible to obtain concrete material on these five contradictions, we could at once gain a very clear understanding of the specific origins of the "Cultural Revolution," its specific course and outcome, and the specific stands of the warring factions. But it is precisely here that the Mao regime has made it most difficult to obtain the facts required. In this way, we have mute testimony on how real these contradictions are and how sensitive the regime is to any probing into them.

Without being able to analyze how these five contradictions were specifically expressed, we are unable to relate the "Cultural Revolution" in a specific way to the very general six contradictions listed by the majority. To deal with the six contradictions in abstraction from the five—in fact without even mentioning the five—becomes a barren exercise not without its overtones of scholasticism.

Let me call your attention to an item in the left-hand column on page 2 that was deleted by the comrades of the majority when they substituted their list of general contradictions. This is the sentence in paragraph three from the top which reads, referring to Mao's foreign policy: "This policy, in essence, expresses the narrow national interests of the ruling bureaucracy in China."

We'll come to this point several times—Mao's foreign policy and its relation to the national interests of the bureaucracy. In our view it is necessary to underline this relationship, whereas the comrades of the majority take a different position. At this point the difference was expressed simply by their removing this particular sentence.

Note the very next sentence: "It has oscillated between opportunism and ultraleftism or combinations of both." I will return to this later, since it came up in the discussion at the congress in another connection. Meanwhile it is worth noting how early we injected the item of the ultraleftism fostered by Mao.

In our opinion, this is one of the most dangerous

aspects of Maoism, since it is least understood by the radicalizing youth. One of our main responsibilities is to make it clear to them.

In the next paragraph of the original text on page 2, the point is made about the responsibility for the break with Moscow. It is clearly stated that the main responsibility lies with Moscow. But it is also pointed out that the Chinese government has some responsibility in the matter; that is, in taking the initiative to deepen the rift.

What has happened in general—in this substitution on page 2 which continues on page 3—is a substitution of general abstract statements of contradictions in place of concrete, specific political characterizations of the policies of the regime.

To continue. On page 3, in the column "Proposed Amendments," we come to the paragraph beginning, "All these contradictions . . ." In the last part of the paragraph, we read the sentence, "In this situation, conditions for a genuine political revolution against the ruling bureaucracy matured."

We, of course, welcome the decision of the comrades of the majority to adopt the position of calling for a political revolution. It could be said to be one of the positive results of the "Cultural Revolution." Before that they avoided taking a clear position on this question.

Let us take the next sentence: "The 'Cultural Revolution' constitutes objectively an attempt by the Mao faction to divert the social forces pushing in that direction from an overthrow of the bureaucracy into a reform of the bureaucracy." In other words, they are of the opinion that Mao is trying to block a political revolution, which was maturing, and trying to carry out a kind of reform instead.

Now they don't say that this was his intention; they say that this constitutes an attempt "objectively." But this is rather obscure. It leaves us with a great big question, what were Mao's subjective intentions? What were his political aims? What was he trying to do consciously, as a political figure, looking at the forces as they stood in China? This is very important to understanding the reasons for the "Cultural Revolution."

Now I go over to page 4, to the second paragraph in the second column: "The more radical line pursued by the Chinese leadership towards revolutionary developments since the beginning of the Sino-Soviet conflict which, on several important questions, brought it nearer to the positions of revolutionary Marxism . . ." Some instances are cited of where this is presumed to be true. This coming nearer the positions of revolutionary Marxism, we are told, "reflects the specific relationship of imperialism and the Soviet bureaucracy towards the People's Republic of China, and the objective impact of the rising tide of world revolution on the Chinese masses."

When we analyze this statement, we run into some interesting things from a general theoretical viewpoint. First, on the statement that the Maoists come nearer to the positions of revolutionary Marxism. (The reference, of course, is nearer than the Khrushchevists.) If the declarations of the Maoists are placed in a scale and weighed against the declarations of the Khrushchevists, the scale no doubt tips in favor of Peking. But this is so abstract that it can be misleading. It is necessary to distinguish revolutionary verbiage and throw this out, since for purposes of determining which comes "nearer to the positions of revolutionary Marxism," only those declarations should be considered that are in correspondence with the actions of the regime. These actions in turn must come "nearer to the positions of revolutionary Marxism" if any validity is to be found in the point.

As soon as we do this, everything becomes more uncertain, or at least more complex. For one thing, the *consequences* of the actions have to be taken into consideration and also placed in the scales.

How much weight should be given the catastrophic defeat of the Indonesian Communist party in placing this item in the scales? Isaac Deutscher considered the defeat in Indonesia to be comparable to the defeat in Germany in 1933. No doubt he had in mind what the consequences would have been in the world if there had been a victory in Indonesia. While Moscow also bore responsibility, Mao's responsibility was much more direct and decisive. The opportunism of the Kremlin was well-known. But Mao advanced his policies and influence as a revolutionary alternative to the Khrushchevists and their line. It is precisely because of his success in *appearing* to stand nearer to the positions of revolutionary Marxism that Mao bears the greater responsibility for the defeat in Indonesia. His guilt is truly colossal and it is out of the question to even raise the question of how "near" he stands to the positions of revolutionary Marxism.

One of the conclusions we ought to draw from this is that the posture of standing nearer to the positions of revolutionary Marxism can be a deadly trap for those who mistake it for standing within the framework of Marxism.

But if it is necessary to assign different weights to the items that are placed in the hypothetical scale, perhaps it would also be well to examine the scale itself. Is it really adequate to the task?

In my opinion, this way of considering the policies of the two regimes is altogether too abstract. It leaves out completely the most important item that must be considered if we are really to determine the relationship between the positions of the two regimes and the positions of revolutionary Marxism. That item is, what is their direction of movement?

Let us take Peking, for instance, and the date of 1963, a rather arbitrary date, but one which is convenient inasmuch as that was the time our movement took a formal position on this question at the Reunification Congress, and inasmuch as the comrades of the majority referred to these formulations during the discussion at the congress.

What has been the evolution of the Maoist leadership since 1963? Have they come nearer to the positions of revolutionary Marxism or have they moved further away? The answer to this is absolutely decisive so far as the immediate point is concerned.

If we judge by Mao's actions and declarations, it is obvious that his own opinion was that the majority leadership of the Chinese Communist party even before 1963 was moving away from Marxist positions. He accused them of having taken the capitalist road. That was why, if we are to believe him, he launched the "Cultural Revolution."

We thus come to the period from the eve of the "Cultural Revolution" to its close. How should we estimate this period? During these years, the cult of Mao reached monstrous proportions; Chinese literature, art and science suffered blows comparable to those in the darkest days of Stalin's rule in the USSR; the educational system was closed down; a murderous, unprincipled factional war was opened up; and the struggle for proletarian democracy in China received fresh blows. Did all this represent a movement on the part of the Mao leadership nearer to the positions of revolutionary Marxism? Is that how we should estimate the outcome of the "Cultural Revolution"?

It is hardly necessary to debate the question any longer in our movement. The comrades of the majority themselves drew the conclusion that what is now required in China is a political revolution. They could hardly have come to such a conclusion if they had not decided that the Maoist leadership moved further away from the positions of revolutionary Marxism, not nearer.

We are thus led to the conclusion that there must be virtually unanimous agreement in the leadership of the world Trotskyist movement that both Peking and Moscow are moving in a direction which, in the past six years at least, has taken them further and further away from the positions of revolutionary Marxism. And it can be added that this view is an accurate reflection of the reality.

Consequently, at best, it becomes rather meaningless to try to measure which of them stands nearer to the positions of revolutionary Marxism. At worst it can be quite dangerous since it can convey the impression to our own ranks that the top leadership of the world Trotskyist movement believes that the Maoist leadership actually stands *near* to the positions of revolutionary Marxism and not merely relatively nearer in comparison with the Khrushchevists as both of them race away from revolutionary Marxism.

From the methodological point of view it is rather deplorable to rest on the statement made in 1963 without taking into account the direction in which the Maoists have been moving since then. Such an approach is static and not at all dialectical.

It might be argued that it is quite true so far as domestic policy is concerned that the Maoist leadership, like the Khrushchevist leadership, has been moving further and further away from the positions of revolutionary Marxism but that this does not hold true for foreign policy, which is the point under discussion.

But this is hardly tenable either. Such a stand would signify a conviction that there is no relationship between the domestic policy of the Mao regime and its foreign policy, or still worse that its foreign policy is the precise opposite of its domestic policy—that while moving further and further away from revolutionary Marxist positions domestically, Mao was moving nearer to Marxist positions internationally.

Such a stand would fly in the face of basic Marxist theory which views foreign policy as merely the extension of domestic policy.

Naturally, if anyone can really *prove* this point, then Marxist theory would have to be reexamined. We suspect, however, that the "proofs" would turn out, on close examination, to be examples of the ultraleftism fostered by the Mao regime in many parts of the world—instances in which it tries to make its pseudorevolutionary mask look more real.

Ultraleftism is not nearer to the positions of revolutionary Marxism than rank opportunism. In certain situations ultraleftism can be more dangerous than opportunism because it is less well understood and because it *appears* to be more revolutionary than opportunism.

Ultraleftism is not always merely a disease of small sectarian groupings separated from the masses and with very little chance of overcoming their isolation. When used by conscious opportunists it should be viewed as preparation for a new opportunist betrayal. An ultraleft turn is very deliberately undertaken by such opportunists in order to undercut a revolutionary opposition or to gain a fresh following to be used for bargaining with reactionary formations. The history of Stalinism provides illuminating examples of this. An ultraleft posture can be extremely dangerous for the revolutionary Marxist movement when it is undertaken by a state power with vast material resources and the prestige of a revolution at its disposal. For our movement, the ultraleftism of the Maoists is a very important question.

The truth of it is that Peking's foreign policy has been oriented to seeking bases of support for the regime in two areas. One is with any national bourgeoisie that cares to enter into a mutually profitable relation with the Mao regime, including the extension of "peaceful coexistence" to domestic class relations. These deals, as we have seen, above all in Indonesia and Pakistan, can reach degrees of opportunism not much different from the opportunism practiced by the Khrushchevists and certainly not different in its disastrous consequences to the revolutionary movement.

The other area where Mao seeks bases of support outside of China is among radicalizing sectors of the population. The Maoists assume an ultraleftist posture which corresponds to the impatience and lack of experience of these sectors, their rejection of the crass opportunism of the Social Democracy and the Kremlin, and their search for an alternative revolutionary leadership and policy.

At the world congress it was implied by some of the comrades who mentioned this point in taking the floor, that if the resolution did not stand on the 1963 statement concerning the Peking leadership being "nearer to the positions of revolutionary Marxism" then this would signify giving up our position favoring China in the Sino-Soviet conflict. It was even implied that it would signify shifting to the position of supporting Moscow in this conflict. This argument was not very well thought out, in my opinion.

In taking sides in an interbureaucratic dispute like this, we base our estimate on what will best advance the interests of the world revolution. Our stand does not necessarily hinge on the policies advocated and practiced by the two sides, although I will agree that it could be a sufficient reason if one or the other of the contending parties were actually to begin moving nearer to the positions of revolutionary Marxism. Unfortunately, in this instance, time and events have shown that neither of them is moving in this direction. Consequently it is necessary to base our stand on other considerations.

While we are dealing with this particular paragraph of the amended draft on page 4, I would like to call your attention to the phrase about "the specific relationship of imperialism and the Soviet bureaucracy . . ."

What this phrase reflects is the opinion that the foreign policy of the Mao regime is in essence determined by the attitude of imperialism, and not by the national interests of the bureaucracy. This is spelled out a little bit more clearly by Comrade Germain in his polemic with Comrade Charlier, which appears in *International Information Bulletin* No. 8 under the title "An Unacceptable Amendment." This has some interesting ramifications but

I will reserve comment on it for the time being as I plan to make a contribution to the *Bulletin* on that particular exchange of opinion.

And then we come to still another phrase, "the objective impact of the rising tide of the world revolution on the Chinese masses." The meaning of this, if I interpret it correctly, is that the Chinese masses, responsive to the rising tide of the world revolution, exert some kind of pressure on the regime to which the regime in turn responds. This raises a series of questions that ought to be answered. In what way does Mao respond to the pressure of the masses? Through what measures and through what institutions? Or, looking at it from a different angle, through what actions and through what institutions do the masses pass the pressure of the world revolution on to the regime? Democratic ways and means of exerting pressure or control by the masses are missing in China. Other means, such as strikes, demonstrations, and slowdowns are not welcomed, to say the least.

How can the masses even voice their opinions in China? It is true that at a certain stage of the "Cultural Revolution," wall posters were permitted. But this was hardly adequate; it was intended as part of a factional maneuver, and it was soon ended. The truth is that critical thought—thought responsive to revolutionary developments abroad—is not allowed in China. Finally, what information do the masses have about events in the world except the information doctored up with Mao Tse-tung Thought that is fed through the Chinese press and radio?

On the same page 4, in passing, note the small addition of the words "in several countries." This was defended at the congress as being one of the improvements added to the document. From our viewpoint, it watered the document down a bit. Instead of stating that the regime followed a policy of collaborating with the colonial bourgeoisie, the document is changed to read that this policy was followed "in several countries"—implying that in other places, it was not followed.

It's not a big point, but it's something to be noted. Was the regime doing its best to follow a consistent policy of collaborating with the colonial bourgeoisie? Or did it happen only in several countries because they were inconsistent in following a revolutionary policy? In other words, did Mao follow a revolutionary foreign policy in general, with only some temporary aberrations in several countries? Such a view may stand in back of a small change like this, even though the modification in and of itself is not a great one.

The final fate of this sentence is not without interest in revealing the thinking behind the small insertion of "in several countries." Here is how the paragraph reads that will appear in the version adopted by the majority for publication:

"In place of conducting a policy stimulating a consistent development of the world revolution, which could have brought new socialist allies into being and carried the struggle for socialism into the main strongholds of the capitalist system, the policy led the Maoist tendencies in Pakistan several times to oppose the mass movements that developed there."

If this final version means anything, it means that Peking sought to follow a policy of stimulating the world revolution but did not do so consistently. This inconsistency led the followers of Maoism in Pakistan into the error "several times" of opposing the mass mobilizations that occurred there.

This comes perilously close to permitting the blame for the results of Peking's opportunism in Pakistan to fall on the local lieutenants of the cult instead of the real criminal, Mao. However, they fell into this error only "several times." Next time they may do better.

It should be observed how the original sentence concerning Mao's following a policy of collaborating with the colonial bourgeoisie was finally washed out.

And notice how the logical sequence of the paragraphs has likewise been washed out. For the one paragraph now ends, saying how the Maoist tendencies in Pakistan several times opposed the mass movements there and the next paragraph begins, "This helped prepare the way for the catastrophe in Indonesia . . ."

I fail to see why this should be listed as an improvement in the document.

This still does not end this point. At the end of the document (fourth paragraph from the end), the comrades of the majority inserted a paragraph which states that Peking's basic policy has continued to "imply" support to whatever bourgeois government in a semicolonial country "happens to diplomatically collaborate with China . . . which leads to disastrous results for the revolutionary class struggle in these countries."

I suppose this is intended as consolation to the minority. It is nevertheless hard to understand why the comrades of the majority would want to subject the plain, simple paragraph in the original to such torture.

Farther down on page 4, the characterization about Peking's prestige and influence having been reduced to "abysmal levels" has been deleted. Again, this is not much. But, in our opinion, the original statement was accurate, if you compare Peking's present prestige with the colossal prestige it enjoyed at the beginning of the Sino-Soviet conflict.

Naturally, if a better phrase can be found to characterize the decline in Peking's prestige, we are for it. But the comrades of the majority apparently were not interested in measuring whether Peking's prestige was nearer or further than an abysmal level, and so left it rather high.

At the bottom of page 4, we come to an interesting substitution. The original notes that after a big campaign against Liu Shao-chi, in which he was branded as a lackey of imperialism, etc., etc., the regime topped off the campaign by itself offering "peaceful coexistence" to Nixon's administration. This created quite an impact in Washington. A great deal of material appeared in the capitalist press concerning the significance of the move. In our opinion, the move was consistent with the basic policy of the Peking regime, which is to express the narrow national interests of the privileged bureaucracy.

But if you do not hold that view of Peking's foreign policy, then the gesture toward the Nixon administration could appear to be merely an aberration, an aberration in a course that is otherwise more or less revolutionary, an aberration that really ought not to be noticed.

This deletion, consequently, was taken by us as a possible indicator of divergent estimates of the Peking regime.

On page 5, you will note that the word "disasters" has been changed to "setbacks." When an observation was made by Comrade Dowson at the congress concerning the consistency in direction of such changes, the majority comrades pointed out that the word "disasters" was left in other places in the document. Thus it appeared that we were being unreasonable in insisting upon the word "disasters." But we would never fight over a single change like this. What interested us was the pattern revealed by the series of changes.

The next change is the shifting of two entire paragraphs over to page 6. We have no objection to a shift of this nature. The phrase "this erratic pilot" was mentioned at the congress by the comrades of the majority as an instance of where the tone of the document was out of keeping with the seriousness that ought to characterize a resolution of this nature, and which they thought it advisable to delete. We do not insist on any phrase like this but it was hard to understand the objection. What Maoist publication does not hail the great chairman as at least a "pilot" or "helmsman"?

Further down on the same page is another change. We are indifferent to this one since it is required for continuity once the previous paragraph has been shifted.

On page 7 what has been changed is the estimate of the role of the army. The original sentence states that during the "Cultural Revolution" the army under Lin Piao served as the ultimate authority. This was changed to "increased authority of the army under Lin Piao." And the "antidemocratic characteristics" of the leadership was changed to "bureaucratic." In this instance we are indifferent to whether the adjectives "bureaucratic" or "antidemocratic" are used, although we are curious as to why such a change was thought necessary.

The question of the weight of the army came up for some discussion at the congress, although not a great deal. In our opinion, the army was, in fact, the ultimate authority during the "Cultural Revolution." The evidence is abundant showing that in key disputes in a number of different places, the force that played the role of ultimate authority was the army. If the army was not the ultimate authority during the "Cultural Revolution," what force was the ultimate authority? The shattered party? The divided bureaucracy? The chaotic Red Guards?

Of more importance is the role of the army following the "Cultural Revolution." For if the army played the role of ultimate authority during the "Cultural Revolution," as it did, then a certain precedent has been set that cannot help but have significance for the succeeding period.

So we must ask, just who is the ultimate authority in China today? Is it the party? The youth? The secret police? The unions? The government apparatus? The educational system? The Red Guards? What force in China today constitutes the ultimate authority if not the army under Lin Piao?

It is already possible to trace a certain rise in the role of the army. Let us recall the report that at the October 1968 plenum of the Central Committee, Lin Piao brought in the army to make sure of a majority for Mao. That was the decisive instrument with which Mao won his majority.

One of the consequences was that at the Ninth Congress of the Chinese Communist party, Lin Piao was designated the heir of Mao. This is perfectly consistent with the role played by the army in the previous period, during the "Cultural Revolution." I don't think that Mao utilized the new constitution to designate Lin Piao as his heir simply as a personal favor to a close friend, no matter what the favors Lin Piao may have performed for him. The designation of Lin Piao as heir was made for political reasons.

Why the comrades of the majority insisted on this change becomes all the more obscure in face of the fact that they let the following sentence in the original stand: "By virtue of its interventions in the conflicts between the contending bureaucratic factions and between the masses in motion and the regime, the army—at the expense of the leading role of the party—has become the mainstay of Mao's rulership, the chief arbiter and principal centralizing force in the country. This is one of the most dangerous consequences of the 'Cultural Revolution.'" That sentence is to be found in the second paragraph on page 8.

How did the army become the "chief arbiter and principal centralizing force in the country" following the "Cultural Revolution" if during the "Cultural Revolution" it did not serve as the "ultimate authority"? It is difficult to follow the reasoning of the comrades of the majority on this point.

To this should be added the fact that on page 9, in the third paragraph from the top, they left the sentence in that reads: "Thus behind the Red Guard movement stood the army as the final authority, sometimes instigating the bands of youth, at other times restraining them or even reversing what they had done." All they changed in that sentence was the word "instigating." They let the phrase "final authority" stand.

Yet at the congress, several delegates scored the way original draft has used the phrase "ultimate authority" in characterizing the role of the army during the "Cultural Revolution."

To finish with page 7. Further down, the one word "episodic" has been deleted. In analyzing the mobilizations, we said they were "limited and episodic." The comrades of the majority did not like the word "episodic." This is a question of estimate. It is my impression that the comrades of the majority conceived the mobilizations as being more continuous during the "Cultural Revolution" than we were able to ascertain them as being. To us it appeared that the regime very early sought to reduce the scope of the mobilizations and to keep them under control so as to be able to turn them off when they had served their designated function. Thus while some large mobilizations did occur—we don't deny that or their importance— they turned out to be episodic, not continuous on a tremendous scale. The sharpness of the civil strife, which led to considerable bloodshed, particularly as the army moved against the strongholds of the opposing main faction, is another question.

On page 8, we come again to the question of the army. Following the sentence I already quoted concerning the army now being the "chief arbiter and principal centralizing force," a sentence notes the "ominous pattern" that has been set for the future. In place of this, the comrades of the majority substituted the assertion that Mao "tends to reduce again this great weight gained by the army during the previous period, by putting the emphasis on the reconstruction of the party as the mainstay of the regime and the necessity of a single central leadership for all power apparatuses."

We were much more cautious. In our opinion, the sentence they introduced implies confidence that that's what Mao intends to do—reduce the power of the army. Against that, you've got to weigh his political relations with Lin Piao, particularly his making the head of the army his heir. In any case, we felt it better to be more cautious about Mao projecting a reduction in the role of the army, at least for the time being.

The next change is a small one—from Mao was "obliged to take" a risk to Mao "took" a risk. The original formulation was consistent with Mao's being in a minority position which thereby obliged him to take a risk in violating the will of the majority. If he was not in a minority, then he would not have been obliged to take the risk. If he had been in a majority, he could have taken the step without any risk. We wouldn't battle about that change. We just don't understand the reason for insisting on changing a sentence that was logical into one that is somewhat illogical.

At the end of the same paragraph, the phrase about Mao initiating a "coup d'etat against the majority leadership" is replaced by a very mild phrase, "reestablish his control over the country." The original designated very specifically what Mao did. In place of this, an abstract formulation was substituted. This leaves unanswered the question, how did Mao reestablish his control over the majority? Was it through a decision of the majority? Through their democratic assent? Just how did it happen? Our impression was that it was through the use of the army in a very forceful way, and thus constituted a coup d'etat against the majority. That seems accurate whether you are in favor of the coup or against it.

We come to the next change. This involves deletion of the whole bottom part of the column and the top of the column on page 9, several paragraphs dealing with the nature of the Red Guard movement and the nature of its rebellion. We, examining the Red Guard movement, came to the conclusion that in order to understand it better—particularly its relation to the radicalization of the youth in the Western countries, and in Eastern Europe and the Soviet Union—it was necessary to note how much it was deliberately inspired and fostered and then shut off by the Chinese government.

The tendency exists in certain sectors in talking about the radicalization of the youth on a world scale to cite the Red Guard movement in China as a magnificent example of what has been happening. It is equated with the rebel movement of the youth in the U.S., France, the Soviet Union, and other places.

We think that this is wrong. We recognize that there was a rebel component in the Red Guard movement; but the mobilization as a whole was different from the mobilization in the Western countries in that it was inspired and fostered by the government, and partly financed by the government. This is a very important element in reaching a correct judgment on the nature of the Red Guard movement in China. It requires us to discount that movement rather heavily as a genuinely rebel formation.

Let us recall that where the Red Guards ran into trouble in "seizing power" they were backed by the army. Where they couldn't carry through in the Maoist way, as called for, the army came in behind them and completed the job. In other places where the Red Guards went too far, the army pulled them back. The army exerted its control in every situation like that.

Finally, we saw that whole vast movement, presumably involving millions upon millions of rebel youth, brought to a halt rather rapidly, and retired from the scene as if they were responsive to orders from above. That isn't a characteristic of a real rebel youth movement. It tends to move in a revolutionary direction despite any promulgations from the Establishment on how they should behave or what they should do.

In our opinion, these were the real rebels in China—the ones who rebelled against being demobilized. But just who were the rebel contingents? Where are they today? These questions are very difficult to answer in the absence of any information. But this should be borne in mind in considering this movement.

In the deletion at the top of page 9 we run into another question. This is in relation to the school situation. Part of the means used to mobilize these millions of youth in China was to shut down the schools. This facilitated getting them into the streets. The teachers were given other employment or different tasks than educating the youth. What did this do to the Chinese educational system?

Our opinion was that this constituted a blow of immense proportions to China. We made this judgment in light of the fact that besides the arms race in the world today, there is also an educational race.

The educational race between the Soviet Union and the United States is well-known. Quite frequently we see estimates of how it is proceeding, who is ahead, what subjects are receiving the most attention in the curricula. You will remember that for a while there was talk about how much attention was being paid to the teaching of mathematics in the Soviet Union in contrast to the United States. This was held to be an example of how the Soviets were winning the educational race, and that there should be some adjustments in the American system to make it possible to catch up.

We know that in the educational field, Cuba is not doing so badly. They have eliminated illiteracy in Cuba, and they're continuing to turn out cadres in various fields on a stepped-up basis. What about China? Here the educational system was shut down for the duration of the "Cultural Revolution." Shut down.

It could be that there was a national emergency of such immense import that it required shutting down the schools and utilizing the youth as a factional battering ram. If that was so, then you must admit that even if it was justifiable, some damage was done to the educational system. But the comrades of the majority simply removed this, and put nothing in its place. So we are left with a resolution that says nothing about this important question.

On the same page 9, there are three other changes. In one, the word "confusion" is eliminated and replaced by something else; "excesses" is changed to "differences among"; "instigating" is changed to "manipulating." We have no big argument to make on any of these changes. We simply note that they follow the same general pattern of toning down characterizations of what the Mao faction did in China.

On page 10 there is another deletion of some importance. The original presented the Maoist view of the "Cultural Revolution," then sought to show that this view of the "Cultural Revolution" was not correct, but fraudulent, and that in contrast to the Maoist presentation of the "Cultural Revolution," what was really involved was a multiplicity of warring tendencies—not just two, but a multiplicity.

This was designed to help lay the basis for rejecting the Maoist claims and for deciding not to support either Mao or Liu Shao-chi. We support a different tendency which, insofar as we can ascertain, does exist in China, is moving towards Trotskyism, and may have conscious Trotskyists within its ranks. This position is developed in the subsequent paragraphs.

I imagine that what the comrades objected to was quoting from Maoist sources to indicate how the Maoists picture the "Cultural Revolution." The phraseology used by the Maoists is not exactly scientific. On the other hand, is there a more accurate way of indicating the picture presented by the Maoists of their "Cultural Revolution?"

On page 11, at the top of the page, two words are added. Again this is a small item that might be presented as purely editorial. The sentence as changed reads: "Neither of the chief factions contending for supremacy within the Chinese Communist bureaucracy is *actually* striving for socialist democracy or has a program of *genuine* revolutionary policies at home and abroad."

Those interested in questions of style might observe how an adjective or adverb can alter the meaning of a noun or verb, even though rather subtly. The two chief factions, we might now conclude, could be striving for democracy, could be striving for revolutionary policies, but from our viewpoint what they are striving for is not genuinely or actually democratic or revolutionary.

Towards the bottom of page 11, the phrase "free general elections" has been changed to "such elections." This, in my opinion, is a good change. I'd accept such a change because the formula originally used could be misinterpreted if you didn't read the whole paragraph carefully. Moreover, it could be torn out of context and an enemy could say, "You see, the Trotskyists are talking about having free general elections in China." What we were really referring to is Mao's promise to have elections on the model of the Paris Commune.

At the bottom of the page, a change has been made in the sentence concerning the composition of the "revolutionary committees" that were set up during the "Cultural Revolution." The original states that the committees were constituted "of individuals handpicked by the authorities." This has been modified to say that they were constituted "by compromise between contending factions, under the supervision of the Mao-Lin Piao hard core."

I really do not know where the comrades of the majority found this kind of information. A compromise suggests that the leaders of the two factions got together, in whatever is the equivalent of a smoke-filled room in China, and made a deal. But there's no evidence that this is what happened. We'll come to this point again.

On page 12, two paragraphs are deleted. The first deals with the damage done to the cultural life of China by the "Cultural Revolution." The other deals with the outcome of the "Cultural Revolution" in bringing to new heights the monstrous cult of Mao.

At the congress, several comrades stated that the resolution ought to say something about the damage done to culture in China by the "Cultural Revolution." None of these comrades appear to have noticed that this point was included in the original resolution and was deleted by the comrades of the majority. It was evidence of a kind to show how difficult the delegates found it to compare the two resolutions. Perhaps some of them did not read the original resolution too carefully; or, if they did, they tended to forget items like this.

In any case, in the final draft, the one to be published, the point is squeezed in as a result of the requests of some of the delegates who favored the majority resolution at the congress. Let me read it: "In the field of culture properly speaking, the Chinese leadership has advanced anti-Marxist positions of a Zhdanov type, defending the notion of 'proletarian culture' and bureaucratically submitting literature, art, and science to the 'party line.'"

The name of Zhdanov—the miserable instrument of Stalin—is used to characterize what was done in China to culture under the "Cultural Revolution." Why the squeamishness that requires such a euphemism? Why are the comrades so reluctant to say what terrible blows have been struck against Chinese culture by Mao carrying on the practices of Stalin?

And why is Mao's gangsterism in this field pictured as if it involved a dispute over the concept of "proletarian culture" when what was involved was a brutal war against China's intellectuals as the opening move in a rabid factional fight?

In our opinion, it is important to speak out on what was done under the "Cultural Revolution" to literature, art, and science. This is one of the most telling examples that can be used in explaining to intellectuals—and to students and workers who are interested in culture—what the difference is between Stalinism-Maoism on the one hand and Trotskyism on the other.

The same goes for the cult of Mao. This should be in the forefront of our propaganda in relation to the Maoists so as to compel them to become increasingly ashamed and embarrassed every time they are compelled to discuss the question in front of an objective audience.

It is a strange polemical method that acts as if China's abomination, the Mao cult, which is patterned on the Stalin cult, and even exceeds it in grotesqueness, should not be heavily scored—as if we were carrying on a dialogue in polite company in which certain subjects are just not dwelt on, and preferably not even mentioned. At least it was like that in polite company until the present generation of rebel youth broke into the parlor. Why should we be demure in telling them our opinion of the Mao cult?

Not to speak out is to bend in the direction of those Maoists who are shamefaced about the cult, but who remain staunch Maoists nonetheless.

At the bottom of page 12 is another small deletion in which the phrase stating that the Maoists are "even more guilty" than their opponents of blatantly revising Marxism has been changed to "as guilty as." We will let this go. Perhaps the comrades of the majority are right about the inadvisability of trying to measure which of the factions comes nearer to the positions of revolutionary Marxism, or which has revised Marxism the most.

On page 14, we return to the question of an alleged "compromise" between the Maoists and "parts" of the main opposing faction, a compromise that was allegedly "initiated when the masses started to intervene autonomously into the struggle and thereby threatened the whole bureaucratic rule."

This is a pure deduction. There is no direct evidence available that I know of that the factions got together and made a compromise making it possible to reach an amicable end to the murderous factional war carried on under the fraudulent title of a "Cultural Revolution."

The word "compromise" suggests equality, or at least a kind of balance of power between the factions. What was more likely involved in a situation of this nature was that certain concessions were made to some of the losers in order to speed up the consolidation of the Maoist victory.

The announcement of the convocation of the Ninth Congress of the Chinese Communist party came after the resolution was written and was thus not taken into consideration in the original draft. The announcement itself, however, rather confirmed that Mao had scored a crushing victory. He felt strong enough at this point to hold the first party congress since 1956.

Why did he feel that strong? Because he had reached a *compromise* with his opponents? That would have signified continuation of the struggle in a new way. That's what a compromise would have meant—deferment of the showdown until another time. It would have meant continuing to operate with the other faction. It is much more likely that Mao conceived the Ninth Congress as a finishing blow, the registration of the complete rout of the other side.

They had already been capitulating. The capitulators were given a certain recognition here and there.

The original formulation, while it does not spell things out—the facts were lacking to do that—fits the situation better than the formulation declaring that a "compromise" was reached between the two factions.

On page 15. The first change from the word "them" to the expanded phrase is acceptable. I count it to be an improvement over the original.

On the same page, a little bit farther down, we came again, as I promised earlier, to the question of foreign policy. The sentence in the original states: "While recognizing that for its own reasons Peking often pursues a more aggressive diplomatic policy than Moscow, the Fourth International also criticizes the opportunism of the Chinese Communist leadership." This has been changed to read: "While recognizing that for its own reasons Peking often advocates a more militant line to its followers abroad than Moscow, the Fourth International also criticizes the bureaucratic centrism of the Chinese Communist leadership."

Two changes have thus been made: *"advocates a more militant line to its followers"* in place of "pursues a more aggressive diplomatic policy than Moscow" and *"bureaucratic centrism"* in place of "opportunism."

Let us take the first change—Mao's diplomatic policy and the line he advocates to his followers abroad. I think two questions are mixed up here. What Mao suggests to members of his cult is not necessarily identical with the regime's diplomatic policy. Even in the case of a healthy workers state the diplomatic policy of the government might be at variance with what the leaders of the revolutionary party in that country might suggest to revolutionists abroad.

Thus this change shifts us from the question of Peking's diplomatic policy to a different subject, the allegedly more militant line it advocates to its followers abroad.

Why this change was made, I do not know. It was not explained at the congress. To strike out mentioning Peking's diplomatic policy could be taken to mean that it is not worth mentioning or that it is of no interest to us.

The substitution is not without its faults in its own right. It could be interpreted as implying that Peking, in advocating a more militant line to its followers abroad, is coming nearer to the positions of revolutionary Marxism.

The insistence that Peking comes nearer than Moscow to the positions of revolutionary Marxism can lead some comrades to conclude that Peking is not only near to those positions but is actually coming nearer or could come nearer. The comrades of the majority, we have deduced, do not hold this position, but they are far from having made this crystal clear. So perhaps we should take a minute or two to explain the consequences of thinking that Peking is coming nearer to the positions of revolutionary Marxism, or could come nearer.

If Mao is capable of projecting a more militant line to his followers abroad, what is to prevent him from projecting a *more and more* militant line? A revolutionary line, or something close to it? If it is really possible, then we should prepare for it.

But then it is ridiculous to call for a political revolution in China. What revolutionists everywhere ought to do, if the possibility is a real one, is struggle to push Mao more and more in that direction. However, that runs counter to the line of trying to mobilize the masses in China to overturn Mao's regime through a political revolution. If Mao can project a more and more revolutionary line, then in the intrabureaucratic struggle between Mao and Liu Shao-chi, we ought to try to form a bloc with Mao in order to crush the danger from the right wing. That would create conditions in which it would be much easier to push Mao further to the left.

Fortunately, the comrades of the majority are completely against any such perspective and reject it out of hand. They stand for a political revolution in China.

It appears to us, however, that there is a certain inconsistency in this stand and the formulations demanded by the majority comrades concerning a supposedly more militant line advocated by Mao to his followers abroad and the supposedly more radical line pursued by the Chinese leadership towards world revolutionary developments. We wondered what concepts they had in mind that led them to insist upon such formulations.

Let's turn to the second change in this sentence on page 15, the change from "opportunism" to "bureaucratic centrism." That seems like a very small change, a tiny unobjectionable change, but it turned out to be one of the points that stood out in the discussion on the "Cultural Revolution" at the world congress.

In his contribution, Comrade Pierre Frank explained that while he was not the one responsible for suggesting the change, he voted for it. In defense of his vote he said that "bureaucratic centrism" was the correct label to put on the policy of zigzagging between opportunism and ultraleftism which the comrades of the minority themselves included in the original draft.

(We would have been willing to settle for the original sentence about Mao zigzagging between opportunism and ultraleftism in his foreign policy. Unfortunately the comrades of the majority deleted it.)

In any case, Comrade Pierre said, in defense of his vote, that the formula "bureaucratic centrism" was used by Trotsky in 1928 in his introduction to *The Third International after Lenin* (Pathfinder, 1936, 1996).

It should be mentioned that a new edition of *The Third International after Lenin* was published this spring in France under the editorship of Comrade Pierre, who also supplied a preface. This edition has been checked against the original Russian manuscript in the Trotsky archives at Harvard. It is an improvement over the old English edition and includes a foreword by Trotsky, written in 1929 after he was exiled from the Soviet Union, which does not appear in the English edition.

In the foreword Trotsky mentions "Stalinist centrism," and he also refers to its zigzag course in foreign policy. He calls Stalin's policies "a variety of the same centrism" as that represented by "Friedrich Adler & Co." but "based on the ideological and material resources of a state that emerged from the October Revolution."

What Comrade Pierre had in mind, I suppose, was not this foreword, in which the term "Stalinist centrism" is used, but the subsequent item in the French edition, a letter written by Trotsky from Alma Ata in 1928, which actually constitutes an introduction to the main document in the book, the famous criticism of the Draft Program of the Communist International. In the English edition, this letter, entitled "What Now?" follows the main document. It is here that Trotsky uses the term "bureaucratic centrism."

What did Trotsky mean by this term? To begin with, I don't think he identified it with zigzagging, although zigzagging is one of its characteristics. For example, Trotsky speaks elsewhere in *The Third International after Lenin* of the "inevitable Leftward zigzags of the Chinese bourgeoisie." Evidently "bureaucratic centrism"—which certainly does not refer to any bourgeoisie—has a deeper content than mere oscillations in policy.

Comrade Peng made what I thought was an effective rebuttal on this point. As he put it, we no longer stand in the period of 1927–28. The situation has changed. As a matter of fact, Trotsky, and the whole Left Opposition internationally, dropped the use of the term "bureaucratic centrism" in reference to the ruling group in the Soviet Union when the orientation of calling for a political revolution was adopted in 1933. Trotsky in 1927 and 1928 had not yet reached the position that a hardened bureaucratic caste had crystallized out in the Soviet Union which could be removed from power only through a political revolution. "Comrade Pierre Frank, of course, understands this very well," Comrade Peng said, "but then he did not explain it."

Comrade Peng maintained that if one believes there is an analogy between the situation in China today and the situation in the Soviet Union in 1927–28, then it is inconsistent to call for a political revolution in China.

On the other hand, if you call for a political revolution in China, then to be consistent in drawing an analogy with the Soviet Union, you must say that the situation in China today is comparable to the situation in the Soviet Union after 1933, or after it became clearly established that a hardened bureaucratic caste had seized a monopoly of power and consolidated its position so firmly that it could be removed only by a political revolution.

For myself, I would like to add a few observations on Trotsky's use of the term "bureaucratic centrism." In 1927–28 he distinguished between the Right, which was intertwined with the growing bourgeois tendency observable in the Soviet Union at the time, the Left, represented by the Left Opposition, which was carrying on the tradition and program of Leninism, and the Center, the key figure of which was Stalin. Trotsky's terminology, as well as his platform at the time, was shaped by the view that the Communist party in the Soviet Union and the Comintern on a world scale could still be reformed. Thus in the letter "What Now?"—which I assume Comrade Pierre was referring to—Trotsky states the position of the Left Opposition as follows:

"In any case, the Opposition, by virtue of its views and tendencies, must do all in its power to see that the present zigzag is extended into a serious turn onto the Leninist road. Such an outcome would be the healthiest one, that is to say, involving the least convulsions for the party and the dictatorship. [Trotsky means the dictatorship of the proletariat.] This would be the *road of a profound party reform, the indispensable promise* [premise?] *of the reform of the Soviet state*." [Emphasis in the English original.]

We can see in this the consistency in Trotsky's use of the term "bureaucratic centrism" and his program of reform rather than political revolution.

This is not the end of the matter, however. In 1935 Trotsky returned to this question and brought things up to date both as to terminology and the great historic analogy he saw between the degeneration of the French and Russian revolutions. He did this in an article entitled "The Soviet Union Today." This was published in English in the July 1935 issue of *The New International* and republished in the summer 1956 issue of the *International Socialist Review*.

Trotsky explains in this article that "bureaucratic centrism" has given way to "bureaucratic absolutism"; or, in relation to the historic analogy he was discussing, "bureaucratic Bonapartism."

In the period 1926–27, Trotsky recalls, the question of the "Thermidorean" reaction was intensively discussed among the opposition circles. A split even occurred over the question. At the time, Trotsky projected the possibility of a Thermidorean triumph only in the future, and even then, of course, only if the growing rightist tendencies in the Soviet Union were not halted. Looking back, he continued, it can be seen that the analogy was used in a faulty way. Actually the Soviet Thermidor began in 1924. And the "Thermidoreans can celebrate, approximately, the tenth birthday of their victory." The present political regime in the USSR, he said, is "the regime of 'Soviet' (or anti-Soviet) Bonapartism, closer in type to the Empire than the Consulate."

Trotsky did not say in his article whether he considered it to have been an error to use the term "bureaucratic centrism" in the earlier period. He was concerned only about correcting the broad analogy with the French revolution; and he said that whatever adjustments this correction might call for, it did not alter the correctness of the program and policies which the Left Opposition had fought for. These had been vindicated completely by events.

We note that by 1929, in his foreword to *The Third International after Lenin*, he used the term "Stalinist centrism" instead of "bureaucratic centrism," and distinguished "Stalinist centrism" as a specific variety of centrism, observing that in distinction from centrism in general, as hitherto seen in the workers movement, it had at its disposal the ideological and material resources of the state that had emerged from the October Revolution. By 1935 he had adopted the term "Soviet Bonapartism."

Whatever we may say today about the use of the term "bureaucratic centrism" in the late twenties, it is clear that the shift to the term "Stalinist centrism" and then "bureaucratic absolutism" or "Soviet Bonapartism" did not signify that the Trotskyist movement had taken the view that the Kremlin could no longer follow a zigzag course. During his pact with Hitler, Stalin ordered a sharp left turn for the Communist parties in the Allied countries. Again in the period following World War II, Stalin finally shifted far enough to the left in Eastern Europe to topple a number of capitalist states.

All of this has an important bearing on our appreciation of the course of the Chinese revolution, but I will leave that for another time.

In relation to the question of using the label "bureaucratic centrism" to designate the bureaucracy in China, Comrade Livio Maitan made the point, if I understood the translator correctly and the translator was translating and not betraying Livio, that the phrase "hardened, crystallized caste" is not a scientific designation. The term "bureaucracy" is meaningful but the term "hardened, crystallized caste" does not signify anything in a scientific sense. I think this relates to Comrade Livio's view that the term "Stalinism" should be reserved for the specific period of the worst excesses under Stalin in the middle thirties, a view I do not at all agree with.

Aside from that, we have used the term "hardened caste" and similar terms to designate the development of the bureaucracy to such a point in a workers state that it completely displaces proletarian democracy and establishes its own rule. In the political arena, we have recognized this qualitative difference from "bureaucratism" in general by calling for a political revolution.

The attitude of the bureaucracy toward political power—towards proletarian democracy—is a certain indicator of the degree to which a caste has been formed. If it succeeds in eliminating proletarian democracy, refusing the masses any possibility to express themselves; if it prevents the formation of independent proletarian tendencies and political parties, you can be certain that it has special reasons for this and that it understands these reasons quite well. The point of qualitative change in the crystallization of this peculiar formation is registered by its success in monopolizing state power, which it then uses to consolidate and defend its special privileges at the expense of the interests of the masses and the revolution.

In comparing the bureacracies in China and the Soviet Union from this standpoint, I would say that differences between the two can be recognized. The Soviet bureaucracy is older, more hardened, more entrenched, with the greater wealth and resources of an advanced industrial power at its command, able to afford a more crass display of opportunism. In other words, a number of differences in quantity or degree can be found—and these are important—but qualitatively, the two formations are pretty much the same. In both instances, we are compelled to call for a political revolution and by that fact we recognize that a certain identity or equivalence does exist despite the differences.

It may seem that I am belaboring the point. But it also seems to be of considerable importance to the comrades of the majority. Even after the discussion at the congress they insisted on their formulation with but a small modification. Here is how it reads in the final draft which is to be published as the majority document:

"While not forgetting that the Chinese leadership is led by the defense of its own interests to inspire among its partisans in the world a more militant line than Moscow's, the Fourth International criticizes the bureaucratic centrist nature of the policy."

We would very much like to know why the comrades of the majority are so insistent on the forty-year-old label "bureaucratic centrist" which Trotsky dropped so long ago.

In the next changes on page 15, several points are involved. We will begin with the question of granting aid to guerrilla forces. In the original, it is indicated, although not stressed, that Peking's chief purpose in this is to create an image to the left of Moscow. In the reformulation, the stress is placed on the objective consequences of granting material aid in this way. Once again the objective consequences of Peking's ultraleftism are left out.

Without a break in the paragraph, the reformulation then brings in Peking's attacks on the right-wing policies of the Communist parties under Moscow's influence, and its attacks on some of the features of bureaucratic rule in Eastern Europe, all of which are described as "objectively" contributing to deepening the crisis of Stalinism and facilitating the upsurge of the new youth vanguard. These sentences replace the sentences in the original, pointing to the fact that Peking's basic policy is "peaceful coexistence," that the leaders of the Chinese bureaucracy are motivated by "narrow nationalistic considerations," that their line is that the revolution must first pass through a "bourgeois stage" before it can reach a socialist stage, that it "counsels and countenances support to bourgeois countries," and does this as a substitute for "mobilizing the masses for uncompromising struggle against the neocolonial regimes."

These points, deleted from the original, appear completely valid to us, both empirically and theoretically. They are completely explainable from a Marxist standpoint if it is granted that what exists in China is a bureaucratic formation so hardened that it can only be broken up by a political revolution.

Of course a problem is created if it is maintained that such a formation does not exist; then it is more accurate to say that what does exist is "bureaucratic centrism."

To stress the objective consequences of Peking's actions at this point is out of place, particularly when it is substituted for something more fundamental to understanding the nature of the regime and the origins of its policies. A clear appreciation is required of the nature of the bureaucracy in China, its degree of development, and its motivations. Otherwise we can run into the error of substituting questions of a secondary order for the more important primary questions, as has occurred in this instance.

It is not enough to point out how some of Peking's actions "objectively" assist the revolutionary process. It is not enough, either, to point out how some of Peking's actions "objectively" aid the counterrevolution, leading to such catastrophes as the one in Indonesia. It is necessary to first grasp the nature of the bureaucracy in China, its narrow, nationalistic interests and preoccupations. From this we can gain a correct and balanced appreciation of the political aims of the leadership of that bureaucracy both domestically and internationally. Then, in the light of the international situation and the contradictory forces in operation on a world scale, we can better determine the portent of Peking's actions and to what degree they must be assessed as objectively revolutionary or counterrevolutionary, or a combination of the two.

Otherwise we can have a bad echo of such disputes as whether the ultraleft phases of Stalin's course did not objectively further the world revolution, or at least come nearer to the positions of revolutionary Marxism than the openly opportunist phases. Or, to reduce things to an absurdity, whether Stalin's publication of the works of Lenin did not objectively help the world revolution.

On second thought, that might not be so absurd. Some circles have maintained that publication of the little Red Book by the tens of millions has had objectively revolutionary consequences. One wonders whether this comes nearer to the positions of revolutionary Marxism than Stalin's publication of the works of Lenin.

In the final sentence in this same paragraph on page 15, you will notice that the substitution by the majority mentions that among the youth vanguard, sympathy for the Maoist positions in relation to Moscow remain deep; and it is asserted that the reason the Maoists have been unable to stabilize any important youth organizations anywhere is because of their "organizational sectarianism and political infantilism." Note that there is no suggestion here of a connection between Peking's policies or the meaning of this important and telling failure. The whole question is reduced to the organizational level. I don't know what is meant by "political infantilism"—but I can't help observing that the phrase comes from the same comrades who considered it a journalistic epithet to describe Mao as an "erratic pilot."

I'll return to this point in a moment.

On page 16, I am sure that no one by now will be surprised at the deletion of the characterization of the Chinese bureaucracy as "nationalistic-minded." Since nothing is offered by way of a substitute, one wonders if it was felt that the Chinese leadership is internationally-minded. Or perhaps something in between, neither completely international, nor completely national. A series of questions arises, in fact, as to how the majority comrades really view the leadership of the Chinese Communist party.

On the very eve of the congress, the national interests of the Chinese bureaucracy came into such sharp conflict with the national interests of the Soviet bureaucracy that shooting broke out in several places along the Sino-Soviet border and hundreds were killed in pitched battles over a patch of land in the Ussuri River.

I was glad to see that in the final draft, the Ussuri battles were mentioned, although the narrow nationalism motivating both sides was not brought out. Major responsibility was placed on Moscow, and the answer of the Chinese was said to have been determined by "bureaucratic interests and prestige considerations" and "in the final analysis" by a "concept"—the concept of "socialism in one country." Perhaps it would have been better in this instance to have stressed what kind of minds function in accordance with such concepts. The word "nationalistic" seems the most appropriate.

On page 16, the entire paragraph concerning the "newly radicalized youth who have mistaken the verbal militancy and activism of the Maoist groups as representing Marxism-Leninism" has been deleted. This deletion is, of course, counterbalanced by the addition on the previous page of a reference to the "political infantilism" and "extreme organizational sectarianism" of the helmsman steering the ship of state in China. Such a meager reference hardly provides us with a high-level understanding of this question.

In trying to win youth who have been leaning in the direction of Maoism, or who have gone through a more intimate experience with this disorienting political current, it is important for our movement to stress both the incapacity of the Maoists to build a youth movement—which is a glaring fact—and the *political* reasons for it; namely, the ultraleftism of Maoism which repels thinking youth after first attracting them, as does the cult of Mao, the ritualistic waving of the little Red Book, and the total miseducation it gives its adherents.

In our opinion, if this particular paragraph required alteration—and we do not deny that it could be improved—it should have been sharpened, expanded, and explained in greater detail. We did not do this in the original because of our objective in drawing up merely a line document, leaving it to the world Trotskyist press to provide the necessary supplementary material in the coming period.

A good example, in my opinion, of what is required is the series of articles by Mary-Alice Waters in *The Militant* examining one Maoist organization, Progressive Labor.

The problem of Peking's initial attractiveness to the youth, which is comparable to the initial attractiveness that Moscow once had to the youth, is a very real one. At bottom it involves the error of identifying the leadership of a workers state with the workers state itself and the revolutionary process that brought it into being.

The resolution on the "Cultural Revolution" required at least a specific reference to the problem of Maoism and the newly radicalized youth, not only because it is related to the "Cultural Revolution" but because it is connected with the major task facing the entire world Trotskyist movement in the immediate period ahead—taking maximum advantage of the extraordinary openings provided by the appearance of a new generation of radical youth.

At the bottom of page 16, we come to another change which likewise can hardly be characterized as unexpected. The phrase "the crystallized bureaucratic caste headed by Mao cannot be reformed" has been altered to read, "also in China, the bureaucracy cannot be removed by reforms." By now, we have become well aware that the comrades of the majority are acutely sensitive to the words "crystallized bureaucratic caste" and do not want such a characterization in the resolution.

In our opinion, this demands explanation. Why shouldn't we use this characterization? What's wrong with it? If China does not have a crystallized bureaucratic caste, what kind of social formation does rule China? And what is the nature of the leadership that represents and defends the special interests of this formation?

It's not an exploiting class—a class like we have in the United States or Mexico or elsewhere in the capitalist world. It's not a mere bureaucracy such as is found in the trade unions. It's not like the bureaucracy to be found in Cuba. So what is it exactly? Is it just to be called "bureaucracy"—bureaucracy in general? Is it not possible to give it a more precise sociological definition?

This is very important from a theoretical standpoint. A series of questions are involved.

If in China we do not have a crystallized bureaucratic caste, which is consciously fighting to preserve special privileges, why is Mao so concerned about maintaining secrecy in China? What has he got to hide? Why all this tremendous apparatus in China to prevent anyone from coming in and seeing what is really happening?

The secrecy in China is even worse, if anything, than it was in Stalin's day in the Soviet Union. There are certain areas in China that no one from the outside, from any party, no matter from what country, has ever seen since the revolution so far as we know. What is the political significance of this? How do we estimate it politically, the fact that a regime in a workers state acts this way?

A closely related question concerns explaining why it is that this regime does not turn to the revolutionists in seeking allies abroad. They turn to either the national bourgeoisie, with whom they seek to make some kind of deal or other along the lines of "peaceful coexistence," or they seek sycophants and paid agents. I leave aside people who are sucked in, the innocents and inexperienced who think that Maoism is revolutionary, the people first becoming radicalized. I'm talking about people in the know.

What kind of ruling group is it that exercises power this way in the world today if not a crystallized bureaucratic caste and its representatives?

This is a real question, not a matter of splitting hairs or engaging in a scholastic exercise. It's a real question, dealing with a real formation. And we have to account for it on a theoretical level as well as meet it politically.

Perhaps you feel some relief at having come to the end of the two documents. I hope that by way of compensation you noticed that the final item concerning the existence in China of a crystallized bureaucratic caste actually involves the question of Stalinism. That was the point we started with, wasn't it? So we have come full circle back to the beginning. Almost like Hegel, isn't it? On a higher level of integration of ideas, I trust.

It at least shows that there's a certain consistency in the logical structure of the original resolution. The same note was struck at the beginning and the end, and actually the end indicated the essential grounding for the position that what is required in China is a political revolution.

What has been indicated by the differences that have emerged between the original draft of the resolution and the modified version submitted by the majority? They are rather important from the viewpoint of seeking clarification and arriving at greater homogeneity in the position of the world Trotskyist movement on the question of the "Cultural Revolution" and the nature of the regime in China.

Let us note some of the main divergences observable in the two documents, without attempting to put them in any kind of order.

1. It's evident that there are different estimates as to the degree of damage done by the "Cultural Revolution." This includes damage done to the educational system and to culture in China.

2. There are differences over the nature of the Red Guard movement. We seek a better differentiation of the tendencies within the movement so as not to foster any illusions about its nature as a whole and so as to be able to see better what component was instigated by the regime and was responsive to it and what component constituted genuine rebel youth.

3. There are different estimates of the role of the military—over the role played by the army in the "Cultural Revolution," its current position in the bureaucratic structure as a whole, and its weight in the regime. We realize that this is difficult to determine in view of the secrecy of the Maoists.

4. There are differences over how the "Cultural Revolution" ended. The comrades of the majority are convinced that it ended in a compromise between the two main factions. We were more cautious about this. We are inclined to conclude that Mao has won a crushing victory which he is now trying to consolidate with the help of widespread capitulations.

There is no disagreement, it should be added, over the instability of the situation and the likelihood of fresh convulsions in the coming period.

These differences will no doubt be resolved rather easily as more information becomes available. However, other differences have emerged that go somewhat deeper. A tentative list of these may prove useful.

1. There are differences over the significance of the cult of Mao. We view the cult as a very serious matter. The comrades of the majority discount its seriousness somewhat. They don't disregard it; they are opposed to it. But in the resolution they tend to discount it and this no doubt reflects their judgment of how much attention should be paid to it.

2. There are differences over the nature of Mao's foreign policy. We think Mao's foreign policy is not revolutionary; that he alternates between ultraleftism and opportunism or combinations of the two and that fundamentally he seeks "peaceful coexistence." The majority comrades do not speak so clearly on this. We are not sure if they think Mao's policy is revolutionary, sometimes revolutionary, or just what. In the resolution they assert that it is "objectively" revolutionary. They appear to dismiss its subjective, or consciously calculated aspects.

3. There are differences, apparently, over the nature of the regime. In our opinion, it represents the interests of a narrow, nationalistic, bureaucratic caste, a bureaucracy of a certain specific character. The comrades of the majority appear to view the regime as "bureaucratic centrist" in the sense of the term used by Trotsky in 1928 to characterize the Stalinism of that period before he reached the conclusion that it could be broken up only through a political revolution.

4. Back of this difference may stand different estimates of the meaning of the term "Stalinism." We consider Maoism to be a variety of Stalinism. Where the comrades of the majority stand on this is not clear to us.

5. To clarify this difference, or possible difference, may require a discussion of the origin of the Chinese revolution and the role played in it by the Maoists. A number of theoretical questions come up, such as explaining how a "Stalinized" Communist party could come to power in China.

Some of these questions have not been probed extensively by our movement. Perhaps it is now requisite for us to go into all this in greater detail. Such a discussion will most likely prove valuable in removing sources of differences that could prove even more troublesome in the future than they are now.

6. It is possible that differences of a political nature could arise in the course of the discussion. These would hinge on what attitude to adopt toward Maoism and could generate a certain warmth in the discussion. I don't think this will occur. Nevertheless, it is worth noting a certain insistence on the side of both the majority and the minority as to the correct attitude to adopt in approaching the Maoist youth. This could adumbrate a political difference.

Our opinion is that it is best to make a sharp delimitation and attack the positions of the Maoists in a vigorous polemic while at the same time seeking to engage them, wherever possible, in common actions. Naturally, in a common action working relations have to be established. But on the political and theoretical level, a sharp demarcation is required, otherwise we can lose our own ranks to the Maoists.

The majority comrades think that this sharpness is unnecessary and even stands in the way of approaching the Maoists for the purpose of recruiting from them. At the congress, the majority comrades constantly referred to the fact that during the May days in Paris, the Maoists were to be found on the "same side of the barricades" as our comrades. Therefore, they maintain, a sharp tone should not be adopted in polemicizing with them.

Beyond this tactical question involving the comrades in Paris in May 1968 we see a much bigger question, the problem of ultraleftism, which goes beyond Maoism—Maoism being only a contributing current, although an important one.

How big is the problem of ultraleftism today? How serious is it to the world Trotskyist movement? What are we going to do about it? There are evidently differences over how we should estimate this. Our opinion is that ultraleftism has made inroads into our ranks in some parts of the world and constitutes a considerable problem.

7. Finally, looming behind all of these differences is the question of how to go about building a revolutionary combat party. In the United States, this concerns us a great deal. We see it in relation not only to the Communist party, which is no longer the great problem it once was, but in relation to the ultraleftism of Progressive Labor, of tendencies in the SDS and other formations, notably the Black Panthers. We have the impression that other sectors of the world Trotskyist movement face comparable problems in their daily work of forging a combat party.

Does unanimity exist on how to solve these problems? Here the test of practice is decisive and we think it would be very fruitful if a better exchange could be reached between the sectors of our movement as to their experiences in grappling with ultraleftism.

In closing, let me indicate where the comrades of the majority think we are in basic agreement and what our opinion is on this.

They maintain that we both agree that a privileged bureaucracy exists in China, and that there is a need for a political revolution.

We think this is a correct judgment in general but that the comrades of the majority are unclear or inconsistent in their characterization of the bureaucracy and still more unclear or inconsistent in relating the need for a political revolution to their view of the bureaucracy and its policies.

They maintain that we both agree that the "Cultural Revolution" represented an intrabureaucratic struggle in which we supported neither of the two main contending factions.

That is accurate in general, in our opinion, but again it appears to us that the comrades of the majority are inconsistent and that various things they argue for really imply offering critical support to Mao in the intrabureaucratic struggle.

They maintain that we both agree that the masses were mobilized in China and that this weakened the bureaucracy. We think that is accurate but we differ on the degree of mobilization and perhaps the degree to which the bureaucracy was weakened by the mobilization.

The area of agreement is substantial and should enable us to undertake an educational discussion without undue friction arising.

Finally, I should like to add that in my opinion this is only the beginning of the process of clarification. We hope for a free discussion throughout the world Trotskyist movement, and we are fully aware of the fact that this takes time.

In the next phase, I trust, we will be able to proceed beyond the necessity of examining two texts that on first glance appear to be almost identical.

THE ORIGIN OF THE DIFFERENCES ON CHINA
By Joseph Hansen

The following is the text of the report made by Joseph Hansen at the Twenty-third Convention of the Socialist Workers Party.

At the recent world congress, Comrade Germain stressed the fact that although various differences had arisen as the international Trotskyist movement sought to formulate its stand on the "cultural revolution," the area of agreement remained broad and substantial.

On this, I believe that Comrade Germain is correct. There is agreement on such key questions as the following:

1. That a workers state exists in China.
2. That it is a deformed workers state.
3. That there is no proletarian democracy in China and no possibility of achieving it under the present regime.
4. That a political revolution is required in China to establish proletarian democracy.

In addition to these very basic points, Comrade Germain is correct in citing agreement among most Trotskyists on two more points:

1. That the "cultural revolution" was essentially an intrabureaucratic struggle.
2. That the mobilization of the masses during the "cultural revolution" weakened the bureaucracy in China.

The common position reached by all sectors of the International on these basic questions is a very real and valuable achievement. It means that the International is assured in advance that in assessing current events in which these issues are involved, its political stand will reflect a virtually unanimous view.

This makes it possible to have a very free discussion on the differences that have arisen.

The differences

The disagreements that appeared at the world congress and during the discussion period leading up to it can be listed as follows:

First, differences over *interpretation* of some of the aspects of the "cultural revolution."

These include the role of the youth, primarily the Red Guard movement; the extent of the mass mobilizations and the degree to which they were kept under control or escaped control; the extent of the damage done to culture, education, and possibly other institutions, such as defense, science, the atomic industry; and, finally the role of the military, or its role since the end of the "cultural revolution."

These questions should give rise to no serious problems, since they will be settled by new events and additional information.

In a somewhat different category is the difference over the emphasis to be placed on the cult of Mao. Everyone at the congress, of course, opposed the cult. The question was what weight should be placed on it in an official resolution of the Fourth International.

Associated with this was the question of what tone to adopt in polemics with Maoists. Here it was a matter of judgment, or practical experience, as to the best way to approach revolutionary-minded youth who have been influenced by Maoism.

In relation to this, it was noted that the problem extends into the International. In a few places losses have been suffered to the Maoists.

At the congress, a related question also came up. How important is the danger faced by the International from the widespread ultraleft mood among the youth? In our opinion this is a rather serious question, one not easily solved. Others held a different view.

Comrade Peng's position

Besides these differences, the position taken by Comrade Peng played a role at the congress. He voted for the minority draft of the resolution on the "cultural revolution," but he proposed that critical support should be given to Liu Shao-chi.

In my opinion, this particular difference was of a tactical order. Comrade Peng held that the Liu Shao-chi group favored de-Stalinization whereas Mao was dead set against it, and therefore the interests of the Fourth International would best be served if Liu Shao-chi won out.

At the congress, Comrade Peng held that the possible opening for the Fourth International in intervening in the "cultural revolution" had been missed. The Liu Shao-chi group had been crushed. Thus the issue was no longer current. Comrade Peng maintained that it is nonetheless of historical interest, and of importance in drawing lessons for the future.

As the discussion progressed, differences of another order began to emerge. These were perhaps more important, in the final analysis, than the points of immediate dispute since they concerned the theory of the Chinese Revolution. The following questions came up:

1. The specific nature of the Chinese Communist Party and the correct label to place on it. Is it a "Stalinized" party? If we call it a "Stalinized" party, what does this do to our basic position on the counterrevolutionary nature of Stalinism?

2. The specific nature of the bureaucracy and the correct label to place on it. Is it a "Stalinist" bureaucracy or just a bureaucracy in general?

3. The specific nature of the foreign policy of this bureaucracy. Is it "bureaucratic centrist" or "Stalinist"? Is its basic objective "peaceful coexistence" or the fostering of socialist revolutions abroad?

Origin of the differences

A clear understanding of the origin of these differences in theoretical appreciation of the Chinese Revolution is very important. It can help set the correct tone for the discussion and keep it at a proper level.

The differences were not injected artificially. They arose through the efforts of the international Trotskyist movement to come to grips with a major domestic development that had worldwide impact—the "cultural revolution."

To have differences over such a development is quite natural and nothing to get excited about in a movement that maintains proletarian democracy.

Some of the divergences can be traced back ultimately, in my opinion, to the first attempts of the leaders of the Fourth International to assess the Chinese Revolution theoretically. During the years in which the movement was split, some of the assessments remained frozen; others underwent modification without the benefit of a fruitful exchange of opinion because of the factional struggle.

The discussion has already aroused lively interest internationally. In the SWP, several comrades, perhaps a little prematurely, at once offered contributions, taking advantage of the opportunity afforded by the preconvention discussion period.

One of these early contributions may have created a rather negative reaction because of its tone. This is the contribution made by Comrade Mike Tormey entitled "China—a Fundamental Difference." (*SWP Discussion Bulletin*, Vol. 27, No. 8.)

I will take it up at this point because of the advantages it may offer in further indicating the frame of the discussion and some of the things that ought to be avoided.

Comrade Tormey's position

Comrade Tormey maintains that the reunification of the world Trotskyist movement in 1963 took place "with two divergent positions on China" without the divergences being "clarified." "The SWP," he writes, "has not fought for its line inside the world movement, and we have compromised our theoretical position on China. The leadership has not carried out its responsibility to the rank and file of either the party or the International, especially to the Chinese section."

Comrade Tormey maintains that "the only reason a discussion is on the agenda today is that the United Secretariat majority wouldn't let us smuggle in our line and rewrote the SWP's document."

Besides "smuggle," Comrade Tormey also uses words like "appeasing" and "obfuscating" in relation to the course followed by the leadership of the SWP. He even finds means of employing words like "dishonest" and "betray."

I hope that any comrades who may feel tempted to answer Comrade Tormey in the same tone will not do so. In a discussion of this nature, it is a mistake to permit oneself to become provoked into arguing on such a level. It is better to try to see what point Comrade Tormey is trying to make.

If I understand his underlying thesis it is that the 1963 reunification was a mistake, that it took place on an unprincipled basis, and that the leadership of the SWP in the intervening six years has conducted itself in an unprincipled way because it did not initiate a faction fight over such questions as the theoretical appreciation of the Chinese Revolution and the precise way it was affected by Stalinism.

Perhaps I am overstating Comrade Tormey's thesis. If this is the case, I hope he will not object to my attempting to answer it just the same. My purpose is to try to help prevent the discussion from becoming diverted into the channels implied by his arguments.

A principled reunification

First of all, the reunification in 1963 did occur on a principled basis. A document was drawn up, codifying the principles on which the reunification took place. No one in the world Trotskyist movement challenged this document at the time and no one has challenged it since.

It is especially to be noted that the Healyites, who were the loudest in shouting that the reunification was "unprincipled" and a "betrayal," never published this document, never made it available to their rank and file, never submitted it to criticism.

The reason for this was that the leadership of the Socialist Labour League could not find any good reason for not accepting the reunification on the basis of this document. Had they published the document at the time, explaining that it had been accepted by the majority of the International Committee, they would have exposed the completely unprincipled nature of their own course—which was first to initiate concrete steps pointing toward reunification, and then to split when they found themselves in a minority in the International Committee on such questions as the nature of the Cuban Revolution.

It is quite true that the movement did not unite in 1963 on a monolithic basis. We are opposed to monolithism. As a political party, the Fourth International reunified in accordance with *political* principles. It would have been wrong to demand agreement on all questions of theory or of historical interpretation, although agreement did exist on the big questions of this nature traditionally associated with our movement.

The main area of disagreement was well known to both sides—it concerned the responsibility for the split some ten years before. Whatever the final determination on that might be, it was the revolutionary duty of both sides to seek to heal the split so as to open up the possibility for united action in taking advantage of a series of exceptional opportunities that had appeared, such as utilizing the favorable repercussions of the Cuban Revolution and participating actively in the Algerian Revolution; and, on the other hand, joining forces against both opportunist and sectarian tendencies that had appeared in some sectors of the Trotskyist movement, notably Ceylon and Latin America (Posadas).

Reunification would also make possible an eventual historic estimate of the split in the most objective way possible and with the least likelihood of injuring the continued unity and growth of the world Trotskyist movement. That could be done only at a later date, in the light of fresh experience and with the old factional lineups liquidated.

This way of proceeding was not only the most rational and objective. It was in the Trotskyist tradition. In the SWP we learned this directly from Comrade Cannon. He learned it from bitter experience—and from the Russians.

An instructive precedent

A similar question, it might be mentioned, came up when Trotsky first reached the position in 1933 that a Fourth International had to be built.

Jean van Heijenoort, one of Trotsky's secretaries, tells the story: "A few voices raised the question: haven't we waited too long? Shouldn't we have recognized the need of a new International much sooner? To this Trotsky answered: 'This is a question we may well leave to the historians.' He was undoubtedly profoundly convinced that the change in policy would have been incorrect several years sooner, but he refused to discuss this question because it was no longer of practical and immediate interest."

This bit of history can be found on page 63 of the new Merit publication, *Leon Trotsky—The Man and His Work* (1969).

Thus we can see that a willingness to leave to the historians questions that are no longer urgent in immediate political practice is not without precedent in the history of the Fourth International.

Naturally, this does not mean that such questions have been buried forever. They can come up in connection with new issues. In that case they can acquire a certain currency; but in a quite different, and, it is to be hoped, more favorable context.

The truth is that among the differences that led to the split in 1953–54, the question of theoretical appreciation of the Chinese Revolution did not play a prominent role at all. It is therefore not difficult to abstract the question of China from the differences that led to the split. It is true that differing theoretical appreciations of the Chinese Revolution existed in those days and that these may have had an indirect relation to the issues involved in the split. But anyone holding that view, if he is to be objective in assigning historical responsibility, should very carefully note what role was played in this by the slowness of the SWP in coming to the position that a workers state had been established in China.

In the SWP we could afford to take our time. As in the case of our analysis of the meaning of the overturn of capitalism in Eastern Europe following World War II, we wanted to be sure that we had thought through all the possibile consequences that might follow from our theoretical conclusions. The delay did not affect any immediate, practical political positions of the party. However, this slowness may have had an adverse effect in the International.

If this was the case, we who were associated with the International Committee would have objected ten years later in 1963, at the time of the reunification, to any demand that we "repent," to use Comrade Tormey's phrase. But then none of the comrades of the International Secretariat displayed the least inclination to demand that we repent, and vow that in the future we would think things through at a faster pace.

At the moment they were faced with a deep division within their own ranks. In 1963, comrades Pierre Frank, Ernest Germain, and Livio Maitan stood on one side, Pablo on the other. Among the questions in dispute was their theoretical appreciation of the Chinese Revolution.

Pablo's turn on China

This internal difference among the comrades with whom we were uniting was of considerable interest. Obviously it was a reflection inside the world Trotskyist movement of the Sino-Soviet dispute.

Pablo had made a decided switch in his position on the Chinese Revolution. He now viewed Maoism as one of the chief obstacles standing in the way of de-Stalinization. This judgment was not without an element of truth, in my opinion.

In trying to explain the nature of Maoism, Pablo had come to view it as a Chinese version of Stalinism. This likewise appeared to me to be not without a certain validity.

But Pablo had gone further than that. To explain Mao's Stalinism, Pablo had decided that a stage of Stalinist retrogression is inevitable in any revolution in a backward country. Perhaps even worse, he had reached the conclusion that Tito's regime in Yugoslavia had developed a correct way of combating this tendency toward degeneration—workers self-management. Thus, as against what had happened in China under Mao, Pablo offered what had happened in Yugoslavia under Tito.

As an immediate practical political conclusion in the Sino-Soviet conflict, Pablo favored opposing Mao and giving critical support to Khrushchev, the de-Stalinizer, who was then the head of the Soviet government. Pablo maintained that to do otherwise would mean giving objective assistance to the worst Stalinist forces in both China and the Soviet Union, the forces utterly opposed to de-Stalinization.

Comrades Pierre Frank, Ernest Germain, and Livio Maitan were up in arms over both the deep-going theoretical conclusions and the political position Pablo had reached. They won a solid majority against him in the congress which they held on the eve of the Reunification Congress.

At the Reunification Congress there was no attempt to plaster over these differences with Pablo. They remained on the agenda for further discussion in the normal course of political life in the reunified International. The same held true for the theoretical appreciations of the Chinese Revolution maintained by the majority of the International Committee insofar as these differed from those held by the International Secretariat.

In relation to China only two political issues had to be decided on—which side to favor in the Sino-Soviet conflict and whether to call for a political revolution in China. The first point was easily handled, since both the International Committee and the International Secretariat already favored giving critical support to Peking. In the united organization, only a small minority supported Pablo's contrary view.

On the second point, each side made a concession. Pending further discussion, the comrades of the International Secretariat agreed to a formulation that included the substance of the position of the International Committee, while the International Committee agreed not to insist on the designation "political revolution."

We thought that this was a good temporary solution inasmuch as it removed the possibility of ambiguity in the political position of the International on this question while permitting the comrades who held reservations to consider it further and to await the test of fresh events. The principled nature of this solution was shown by the complete agreement on the specific points drawn up as a political platform in the struggle for proletarian democracy in China.

The reunification of the Fourth International made it possible for us to look forward to future discussions on this and other subjects within a reasonable time that would lead to still greater homogeneity of views.

Fresh splits

The prospect of a strengthened International did not meet with universal approval. On the side of the International Committee, a minority headed by Gerry Healy refused to join in the reunification, deciding instead to split from the world Trotskyist movement.

On the side of the International Secretariat, a minority headed by Juan Posadas had already split for much the same reasons as those motivating Healy.

Before long, Pablo followed their example.

All three of these groups, of course, were strong advocates of democratic centralism. They also practiced democratic centralism quite vigorously—so long as they remained in the majority. As a minority, however, they found many reasons for not practicing what they preached.

Some changes inside the SWP since 1963 should likewise be noted. A few who agreed with Healy—Wohlforth and Robertson among them—found it impossible to abide by the rules of democratic centralism. A few others, who took an uncritical view of Maoism, lost interest in further internal discussion and left the party.

Thus, since 1963, the situation within the International and the organizations in fraternal sympathy with it has altered in various ways. One of the most important has been the addition of sizable new forces through the recruitment of youth.

So far as the composition of the movement is concerned, the discussion today takes place in quite different—and, in my opinion, much more favorable—circumstances than existed in 1963.

In addition, some major events have provided fresh material. These include the deepening crisis and decomposition of world Stalinism, particularly the further sharpening of the Sino-Soviet conflict, the catastrophe in Indonesia, and the big convulsion in China called the "cultural revolution." These developments greatly facilitate a fruitful discussion.

I hope that this is sufficient to answer the question that appeared to be implied in Comrade Tormey's contribution concerning the procedure followed at the Reunification Congress in 1963.

I should like to turn now to a couple of points which he makes that are more directly related to the differences that have arisen over the "cultural revolution."

Question of Liu's program

Comrade Tormey maintains, if I understand him correctly, that the refusal of the SWP to support Liu Shao-chi amounts to "appeasing" the majority of the United Secretariat in questions of principle relating to the Chinese Revolution.

In the effort to substantiate his case, he ascribes to Liu Shao-chi a program that is very far to the left. The method followed by Comrade Tormey in this is hardly a model of objectivity. In the fall 1966 issue of the *International Socialist Review,* in an article on the "cultural revolution," Comrade George Novack wrote that from the accusations lodged against the dissident intellectuals and from other sources, it was possible "to discern the vague contours of their criticism and the trend of their thinking." Comrade Novack drew the conclusion that if the points he listed were taken together, "these positions would constitute a serious oppositional program to the policies of the Peking leadership."

Comrade Tormey assumes that this *was* the program of the Liu Shao-chi faction. As Comrade Tormey puts it, "Comrade Novack has obviously outlined part of the program of the Liu Shao-chi faction."

This may be obvious to Comrade Tormey, but George Novack did not draw that conclusion. He stated that the list represented the "vague contours" and "trend" of thinking of the opposition as a whole. He did not say that this was the program of Liu Shao-chi.

It is not accurate to say that we were "neutralist" in the factional struggle. With our call for a political revolution, for the establishment of proletarian democracy, we stood in opposition to Mao.

But it is accurate to say that we did not offer critical support to Liu Shao-chi, although we defended his right to be heard. There was good reason, in our opinion, for not supporting Liu Shao-chi. So far as we were able to judge from the available information, Liu Shao-chi did not represent the most radical trend. He did not even organize a faction on a declared program in opposition to Mao.

To the left of Liu Shao-chi

In contrast to the readiness with which he ascribes a serious oppositional program to Liu Shao-chi, Comrade Tormey dismisses out of hand any possibility of a tendency in China moving toward Trotskyism. "This position of Comrade Hansen's," he says, "is totally off the wall."

I have the impression that Comrade Tormey did not take time to think this through. If no tendency exists to the left of Liu Shao-chi, and if Liu Shao-chi nevertheless advanced a quite revolutionary program, then we are compelled to conclude that Liu Shao-chi took this progressive step on his own volition. That means that Liu Shao-chi is consciously a revolutionary Marxist or very close to it. Since he originated in the bureaucracy, and was in fact considered for many years to be Mao's chosen heir, and still represents a wing of the bureaucracy, then we have to say—if Comrade Tormey is right—that at least part of the bureaucracy carried out self-reform under the leadership of Liu Shao-chi.

Suppose that similar reasoning were applied to developments in the Soviet Union—that no tendency stands to the left of Khrushchev. Would not the logical conclusion be that Khrushchev represents a tendency in the Soviet bureaucracy moving toward self-reform?

Comrade Tormey, I am sure, will agree that Khrushchev's policy of de-Stalinization consisted not of self-reform of the bureaucracy but of granting concessions to the masses under the pressure of a rising mood of opposition that could easily foster Trotskyism. In the case of the Soviet Union, I am sure that Comrade Tormey would agree that we were fully justified in assuming that groupings could form under these conditions that would gravitate toward Trotskyist positions; that perhaps they had already formed, at least in an embryonic way, and that genuine Trotskyists might already be found in their ranks.

Why weren't we justified in taking a similar attitude toward the situation in China during the "cultural revolution"?

Comrade Tormey, however, insists that we support Liu Shao-chi unless we can tell him specifically whereabouts in China a more revolutionary tendency exists and what its program is.

All we can say in response to that demand for empirical proof is that Mao's totalitarian method of rule and the wall of secrecy he maintains around China preclude any easy access to such information. We must confine ourselves pretty much to indirect indications that tendencies to the left of Liu Shao-chi do exist.

However, I can call attention to three specific items of unusual interest in this connection.

In Mao's prisons

The first is a couple of paragraphs in the article by George Novack in the fall 1966 *International Socialist Review* which Comrade Tormey evidently overlooked. The paragraphs are from a report by a veteran Japanese Trotskyist leader. He explains that one of the reasons for the militancy of some of the adult leaders accused by the Mao regime of being counterrevolutionists is the resistance of many young men and women for a number of years.

"We should not forget the existence of many victims of the 'Great Leap Forward' and other affairs," writes this Japanese Trotskyist leader. "Each one of these has involved thousands of young men.

"We know of one prison alone in the suburbs of Peking where hundreds of youthful political prisoners have been doing heavy labor for many years, resolutely refusing release on the condition of recanting. They are not Trotskyists, at least they do not call themselves such. (Many Trotskyists who were arrested in 1949 and later also remain in prison.) Many Chinese youth and students know of their existence and resistance."

The second item is a very brief report carried by Agence France Presse January 22, 1967, that Kang Sheng, a member of the Standing Committee of the Chinese Communist Party, had been attacked in wall posters for protecting "a Trotskyite student, Tan Li-fu, arrested in December."

We reported this item in the February 3, 1967 issue of *World Outlook* and commented at the time on its possible meaning.

The Sheng Wu Lien tendency

The third item is from the most recent issue (June–July) of *International Socialism*, published by the state capitalist tendency in Britain. Tony Cliff, the leader of this tendency, has this to say:

"In *IS* 29 (Summer 1967) I wrote an article on the Cultural Revolution in China; 'While there is without doubt a "Bukharinist" wing in the Chinese Communist Party, and a Stalinist (Maoist) wing . . . there is *not* a Trotskyist or Left-Oppositionist wing.' I added, however, as the final sentence of the article 'The crises from above may also spur on a new, revolutionary working-class movement below.'

"Much sooner than anyone expected, echoes of just such a movement reached our ears."

Tony Cliff cites a speech made by K'ang Sheng, the minister of public security. (I don't know if this is the same Kang Sheng who was accused the previous year of protecting a "Trotskyite" student.) On January 24, 1968, K'ang Sheng attacked a grouping called "Sheng Wu Lien"—which is the shortened form of "Hunan Provincial Proletarian Revolutionary Great Alliance Committee." This committee was composed of more than twenty organizations. According to K'ang Sheng, it was organized on a declared program that claimed that the "cultural revolution" had remained merely reformist up to this point.

"It may be seen from an article by Yang Hsi-kuang," said the minister of public security, "that they have probably collected some counter-revolutionary works of Trotsky . . ."

Tony Cliff writes further: "At last one of the documents of the Sheng-wu-lien, entitled 'Whither China?' came into our hands." In his opinion, it resembles the manifesto issued by Kurón and Modzelewski in Poland, and Tony Cliff concludes from this that "it is clear that the struggle against Bureaucratic State Capitalism as well as monopoly capitalism is really a world-wide struggle." For the benefit of readers of *International Socialism*, he published four pages of extracts from the document "Whither China?"

We were able to obtain a copy of the complete text of this document as well as the speech by K'ang Sheng, the minister of public security, plus several other items on this subject, including a short speech by Chiang Ch'ing, the wife of Chairman Mao, and a copy of the program of Sheng Wu Lien.

From this material, I would judge that Tony Cliff is overly optimistic in concluding that this is a state capitalist tendency. It could just as well represent a tendency that is seeking to take some of Chairman Mao's proclamations to their logical conclusion, such as demanding that the state machine be smashed and a Paris Commune type of state be established. Some of the formulations, however, read as if they had been written by someone familiar with at least some of Trotsky's writings or the writings of his Chinese followers.

I am of the opinion that more material of this kind will eventually turn up. But this ought to be sufficient to indicate that there is substance to the view that tendencies to the left of Liu Shao-chi did appear during the "cultural revolution."

A tactical question

Before leaving this point, it ought to be noted that the Sheng Wu Lien grouping did not offer critical support to Liu Shao-chi. Instead it offered critical support to Mao Tse-tung.

This should serve as further confirmation of the dangers involved in trying to determine from afar what is the best tactical course to follow in a situation so complex as the one in China and with so many unknowns. Such decisions should be left to the comrades directly involved in the field of action.

Perhaps Comrade Tormey can be persuaded to adopt this view. He says that if a new tendency moving toward Trotskyism actually exists in China, then "Naturally, it would be automatic to support such a tendency . . ."

What if this tendency thought it was tactically advisable to offer critical support to Liu Shao-chi? In my opinion, the best course for the world Trotskyist movement would be to back them up in their judgment. And what if this tendency thought it was tactically advisable to offer critical support to Mao? Would not the same considerations impel us to back them in that even if we held reservations as to the correctness of their judgment?

The question is one of tactics, not principles, during a certain stage of the struggle for a political revolution in China to establish proletarian democracy.

I would like to turn now to a different aspect of the question—our theoretical appreciation of the Chinese Revolution.

This was not on the agenda at the world congress, but the debate touched on it and there can be no doubt that the logic of the discussion is to move in that direction.

Real origin of the difficulties

In his contribution "Thoughts on the History of the Chinese Revolution and the Present Discussion of Maoism," (*SWP Discussion Bulletin*, Vol. 27, No. 8), Comrade Jan Garrett lists three traps which he warns that we can fall into if we just "muddle along," as he thinks we have, on the question of the Chinese Revolution.

He calls these the "objectivist" theory, the "accident" theory, and "eclectic dualism."

The labels are attractive. However, I think they are rather arbitrary.

I have the impression that Comrade Garrett reached his conclusions on this point by mistaking the origin of the difficulties. He appears to assume that the source is to be found in theoretical incompetence or ignorance. I deduce this from his assertion that many SWP members have been just muddling along on the question of the Chinese Revolution. He misses the mark because he does not refer to the real origin of the difficulties.

At the time of the victory of the Chinese Revolution over Chiang Kai-shek and his imperialist backers, our movement was confronted with the necessity to explain the contradiction between certain long-held theoretical postulates and the actual course of events. The postulates were as follows:

1. The peasantry as a class cannot lead a revolutionary struggle through to a successful conclusion.

2. This can be achieved only by the proletariat.

3. The proletariat cannot do it except by organizing a revolutionary Marxist party.

4. Stalinism does not represent revolutionary Marxism; in essence it is counterrevolutionary.

5. Stalinism represents a temporary retrogression in the first workers state; the advance of the revolution will doom it and it will not reappear.

Despite these postulates, which appeared to have been thoroughly established by both weighty theoretical considerations and a mountain of empirical evidence, in the Chinese Revolution the proletariat did not play a leading role as a class. Instead, this role was assumed by the peasantry.

Moreover, no revolutionary Marxist party was formed on a mass scale. Instead, a Stalinist party stood at the head of the revolutionary forces and came to power in a struggle that ultimately toppled capitalism.

Finally, Stalinism was quite consciously cultivated by the new regime. Today this school of thought has culminated in a cult of the personality that if anything has outdone its model in the Soviet Union.

The problem that faced our movement was to explain these contradictions and to determine what lessons should be drawn and what they portended for the future.

So far as the *political* positions of the world Trotskyist movement were concerned, no problem existed. Without exception our positions were correct, ranging from full support to China, despite Chiang Kai-shek, in the struggle against Japanese imperialism to full support for the revolution against Chinese capitalism and the vestiges of feudalism despite the Stalinist nature of the leadership that was thrown to the forefront.

It is very important to remember this, for it constitutes the most positive kind of proof that our movement is a dynamic political formation and not a church dedicated to maintaining the purity of a set of dogmas. One can feel proud in reading the political platforms presented in the documents of that time. They were very good, standing up remarkably well under the test of events.

Problem of the proletarian content

As to the attempts to find solutions to the contradictions between the reality and our theoretical postulates, some of these were clearly in error from the beginning. Others have not held up, or only created fresh difficulties.

In the main, the attempted solutions centered around locating the proletarian content which it was felt must lie at the heart of the Chinese Revolution despite its strange forms and the role of Stalinism.

For instance, in the case of the peasantry, there was speculation that perhaps its true nature had been misjudged. Unlike the peasants of Western Europe and elsewhere, perhaps the Chinese peasants had achieved a proletarian or even socialist consciousness either because of the peculiarities of China's historic background or because of the impact of imperialism on the country.

A current example of this line of thought is to be found in Comrade Moreno's contribution in *Fifty Years of World Revolution*.

Much greater attention was paid to the nature of the Chinese Communist Party. This was only natural since our movement from its very inception has considered the question of the party to be primordial in the process of bringing a revolution to victory. Thus it appeared that the key to the success in China must be sought in the nature of the Chinese Communist Party.

One line of speculation was that Trotsky had made a mistake in concluding that the Chinese Communist Party under Mao had become a peasant party.

Another was that if Trotsky had been right in his conclusion at the time, then it must have changed back into a proletarian organization.

Comrade Morris Stein argued, for instance, if I recall correctly, that there was a steady flow of workers from the cities who went into the countryside and joined the Chinese Communist Party. Their influence, he thought, was sufficient to give a proletarian character to the party.

Another line of speculation concerned the personal qualities and influence of Mao Tse-tung. Some comrades felt that despite everything, when Mao Tse-tung was faced by the supreme test, he had adhered in practice, if not in program, propaganda, or diplomacy, to revolutionary Marxism.

Still another variant was that the very Stalinism of the Chinese Communist Party gave it a proletarian character. The line of thought here was that Stalinism is connected with the workers state in the Soviet Union and that this association therefore makes it proletarian.

At bottom, this view represents an *identification* of Stalinism with the workers state. It is quite a change from Trotsky's position that Stalinism stands in *contradiction* to the workers state, that it is a cancerous growth. As against the *proletarian* tendency represented by Leninism and the Left Opposition, Trotsky considered Stalinism to be *petty-bourgeois* in nature.

Another line of thought, flowing in the same general channel of trying to find something proletarian about the Chinese Communist Party, was the view that this party changed from a peasant party to a "centrist" party, then a "left centrist" party, then an "opportunist workers party," and finally a "workers party."

In the current discussion, the view that Mao's policies should be designated as "bureaucratic centrism" may fall within this frame. At the world congress Comrade Pierre Frank argued for the latter point. Through an error in translation I was under the impression that someone else had introduced the amendment to this effect in the resolution on the "cultural revolution." But Pierre has written me since then that he was the one who suggested it.

While I am on the point, I should like to say that I fail to see what is gained by this nomenclature. If we ask what is the class nature of "centrism," whatever its variety, we are compelled to say that it is petty-bourgeois. That is also the class nature of Stalinism. It is petty-bourgeois.

Thus the introduction of the general term "centrism" does not help in answering whether a Stalinist party can become a revolutionary party. It merely suggests a succession of stages in which the class essence of the gradation or series of steps remains obscure.

Marcy, Swabeck, Posadas, and Healy

It was quite clear from the beginning that all these tentative answers to the central problem carried implications that could prove quite dangerous politically; and we were soon to experience repercussions in our ranks. I will mention some of them.

Sam Marcy and his group rapidly came to the conclusion that Stalinism in power equals a workers state. Since a Stalinist party had gained power in China, this signified that a workers state had been established.

From this position, Marcy evolved into a Maoist of such fervor that he was capable of swallowing even the new constitution, announced at the Ninth Congress of the Chinese Communist Party, designating Lin Piao as Mao's heir.

The consistency with which the Marcyites identify Stalinism with a workers state was shown in the most striking way during the Hungarian uprising when they offered critical support to Khrushchev in using Soviet tanks and troops to crush the proletarian rebellion.

The Marcyites adopted the same position in relation to the current invasion and occupation of Czechoslovakia. They even went so far as to help the Kremlin in its efforts to find a propagandistic cover for crushing the upsurge that was pointing in the direction of a political revolution in Czechoslovakia.

Later in the SWP, we had the sad case of Arne Swabeck, one of the founders of the American Trotskyist movement, who proceeded from the theoretical position that only a revolutionary Marxist party can lead a successful revolution. Inasmuch as the Chinese Revolution was successful, he concluded that the Chinese Communist Party must have been a revolutionary Marxist party, and he ended up as a Maoist.

Juan Posadas followed a similar line of thinking, but with an odd twist. Because of Mao's supposed receptivity to genuine Marxism, Posadas came to believe that Mao derived his finest thought from reading the speeches and writings of J. Posadas. Just how this was accomplished was never made quite clear. Perhaps Posadas believed that Mao had set up a Latin-American Bureau in Peking that occupied itself with translating Juanposadas Thought into Chinese ideograms so that Chairman Mao could imbibe at this fountain.

The identification of Stalinism with a workers state took a different and perhaps still more remarkable twist in the thinking of Gerry Healy. He maintains that there are two, and only two, roads to a workers state—either under the leadership of a Trotskyist party or under the leadership of a Stalinist party.

Thus in the case of Cuba, Gerry Healy refuses to recognize the existence of a workers state because the revolution was headed by neither a Trotskyist party nor a Stalinist party.

Wohlforth lays it on the line

If you wish proof of this aberration, it has conveniently been made available in the most recent issue of the *Bulletin* (August 26). On pages S-5 and S-6, Tim Wohlforth, who seems to have displaced Cliff Slaughter as Healy's chief apologist, explains this remarkable theory.

In Eastern Europe, he says, "The very process of expropriation of capital in these countries was accompanied by a process of the creation of this workers' bureaucracy through the taking over of the government by a workers' party, the Communist Party, and the purging of the government of all forces unreliable to the tasks this party had to carry out—some positive social tasks as well as reactionary tasks."

Wohlforth continues: "The Castro government is in no sense a workers' bureaucracy. In fact Castro has carried out a series of purges against even Stalinist elements within his government—as illustrated by the two Escalante affairs—and maintains complete control in the hands of the petty-bourgeois nationalist forces who came to power with him."

Then Wohlforth gets down to the nitty gritty: "In Cuba, and only in Cuba, the nationalizations were not accompanied by the emergence of a government controlled by the Stalinists."

We hardly need any further enlightenment from this Healyite theoretician. His position is that if the process that actually occurred in Cuba had been led by a Stalinist, say Blas Roca or Aníbal Escalante, then the Healyites would have at once agreed that a workers state had been established. If Blas Roca or Aníbal Escalante had purged Fidel Castro and Che Guevara this would have been proof positive.

But since the Stalinists in Cuba were outflanked and bypassed from the left by fresh revolutionary forces, the Healyites find it incompatible with their dogma to admit that a workers state has been established there.

It is this reactionary theory that has led the Healyites, out of concern for consistency, to commit such abominations as to call Castro another "Batista," to offer critical support to Cuban Stalinism when Castro became alarmed at the growth of bureaucratism, and to speculate, as they did openly in their press after Che Guevara left Havana in 1965 for another "assignment," that Castro had murdered his comrade-in-arms.

Now for the icing on the cake. The Healyites make a great show in their press of alertness to the danger of succumbing to Stalinism. However, they have not set a very good example in practice. Besides succumbing to the temptations of Stalinism in Cuba, they succumbed in China.

During the "cultural revolution," the *Newsletter* suddenly blossomed with rave articles about Mao's Red Guards. It was quite a sight to see the great red banner of Maoism lifted high in the *Newsletter*. This lasted but a short time. Praise for Mao's Red Guards vanished as abruptly as it had appeared. For the past two years, the *Newsletter* has hardly mentioned the "cultural revolution."

What happened? No explanation was ever offered. I suppose that the headquarters gang managed to get the ailing author of the articles back into a straitjacket and that was that. It never occurred to them that he was only acting in strict consistency with Gerryhealy Thought.

Four main results of war

The world Trotskyist movement never landed in such blind alleys as the ones in which Marcy, Swabeck, Posadas, and Healy are now to be found. At the same time, I think it is just to say that we have not yet achieved a fully satisfactory unified theory.

Perhaps we are now in position to accomplish this. With good fortune, this may be one of the outcomes of the current discussion.

The method we should follow is that of historical materialism—not the "objectivist" theory, the "accident" theory, or "eclectic dualism." Studies pursued in accordance with the method of historical materialism are the most likely to bring solid results. So let us look at the process that brought into the world the second generation of workers states.

World War II had four main consequences: (1) the victory of the Soviet Union; (2) the weakening of world capitalism as a whole; (3) the resulting temporary strengthening of Stalinism; (4) an upsurge of revolutionary struggles in both the imperialist centers and the colonial areas.

These four results shaped the course of history for some time, above all the advance of the world revolution.

Eastern Europe

In the case of the East European countries that were occupied by the Soviet armies as they moved toward Berlin, the overturn of capitalism in those areas was explainable as a direct consequence of the victory of the Soviet Union over German imperialism.

The armed struggle was carried on by the Soviet armies and the resistance movement operating in conjunction with them. The capitalist governments collapsed as the Soviet troops advanced. They were replaced by governments in which Moscow, standing behind local Stalinist parties, exercised power.

For a time the Kremlin retained the capitalist structures in Eastern Europe, evidently as bargaining pieces in trying to reach some kind of world settlement with Western imperialism.

When this bid was turned down and Washington opened up the Cold War, Stalin responded by destroying the capitalist structures in the countries occupied by the Soviet armies.

Imperialism was too weak to block the overturns. Naturally, there was a great hue and cry. But no capitalist country in Europe had the armed forces required to push back the Soviet armies. Even the

U.S. armed forces were disintegrating.

The economic forms that replaced the capitalist structure in Eastern Europe were patterned on the economic forms in the Soviet Union. The structure of the state was likewise based on the Soviet model.

The proletarian element in these newly set up workers states clearly derived from the economic forms that were "structurally assimilated," to use the descriptive phrase applied by the comrades in Europe at the time.

The source of the reactionary Stalinist element, that is, the totalitarian political forms, was the Kremlin bureaucracy, the parasitic ruling caste which was keenly alert to the need to set up a replica of its own formation in these satellite states. Possible sources of political dissidence were handled with frame-up trials and purges.

We, of course, favored the overturns in Eastern Europe although we were absolutely opposed to the means used. To us, the overturns constituted fresh proof that the October Revolution was still alive. Stalin had not succeeded in destroying the foundations of the workers state. Despite himself he had had to export Soviet property forms, if only as a defensive measure against imperialism.

At the same time we were fully aware that the basic policy of the Soviet bureaucracy was "peaceful coexistence" with imperialism and that in accordance with this policy Stalin had once again, during these very same years, betrayed the big revolutionary upsurges in Italy, France, and elsewhere.

Yugoslavia

Let us now consider Yugoslavia. Here again, the Soviet victory was the decisive element. This victory served to inspire the Yugoslav people who had already become armed during their struggle against the German occupation.

The Yugoslav Communist Party had played an auxiliary role in the Soviet military defense by organizing the resistance in Yugoslavia against the German occupation and by pinning down German forces through guerrilla warfare. The armed struggle in Yugoslavia was thus linked to the victories of the Soviet armies.

But the Soviet armies did not play a direct role in Yugoslavia as they did in countries like Bulgaria.

British and American imperialism sought to counter the government set up by Tito by bolstering the forces favoring the monarchy. However, they were too weak to succeed in this, even with the connivance of Stalin. The armed forces under Tito smashed the counterrevolution and became the sole real governing power in Yugoslavia.

This government, in turn, took the steps ending capitalism in Yugoslavia. The economic forms that replaced capitalism were modeled on those in the Soviet Union.

In the political arena, Tito, in true Stalinist style, crushed all dissidence or what might appear to be a potential source of dissidence from the left.

Although the independent role played by the Yugoslav Communist Party under Tito was much greater than that of the Communist parties in countries like Rumania and Czechoslovakia under the Soviet occupation, the basic pattern of the process that ended in the establishment of a deformed workers state in Yugoslavia was the same.

Let us turn now to China. The main condition for the peculiar form which the revolutionary process took there was the same as in the East European countries and Yugoslavia—the victory of the Soviet Union in World War II.

The two other conditions following from this one were likewise the same—the weakening of world capitalism and the temporary strengthening of Stalinism.

As for the revolutionary upsurge touched off by the course of the war and its outcome, this occurred on the colossal scale of the most populous country on earth.

As in Eastern Europe and Yugoslavia, the Soviet armies played a certain role by their proximity in the final stage of the war against the Japanese imperialist aggression, but to a lesser degree than in the European theater.

There were other differences, some of them of an unexpected nature.

China's historic pattern

I should like to suggest that the first of these was the strong resemblance of the opening phases of the third Chinese revolution to the revolutions of former times in Chinese history.

The earlier revolutions followed a cyclical pattern. When the exploiting classes in China reached the point of exerting intolerable oppression on the masses, the entire economic system tended to break down. The remarkable canal system upon which so much of Chinese agriculture depended fell into disrepair. It became increasingly difficult to feed the population. Famines began to occur. The central authority became increasingly hated. Finally, the peasantry, goaded to desperation, began to link up, and, more importantly, to organize for battle.

A phase of armed struggle opened, with its guerrillas, focal centers, and peasant armies. Eventually these armies conquered, and a new government, headed by the leaders of the insurgent armies, came into power.

The new government at once went to work to repair the ravages of the civil war, to reduce the exploitation of the peasants, to divide up the land at the expense of the former landlords. The canal system was rehabilitated and extended, once again assuring a dependable supply of food for the population.

The army hierarchy that constituted the new government naturally soon displayed concern for its own comfort, ease, and even modest luxuries. The hierarchy developed into a privileged bureaucracy. The land became concentrated once again in fewer and fewer hands and the new dynasty came to represent the new landlords. The oppression of the peasantry became worse and worse and the system began to break down once again.

The most interesting part of this ancient pattern is the way the peasants succeeded in uniting and building armies imbued with a central political purpose and capable of smashing the old regime and putting a new and better one in power.

A comparison of this phase of the old pattern with the first stages of the third Chinese revolution would, in my opinion, prove highly instructive.

For one thing, it should help counteract the compulsion felt by our movement for so long to find some kind of proletarian quality in the Chinese peasants to account for their remarkable capacity to create a peasant army imbued with revolutionary political aims.

In any case it would make a very good research project for some young Trotskyist theoretician. So much for that point. We come now to more important items.

New world context

Upon achieving their victory in 1949, the peasant armies of the third Chinese revolution were, of course, confronted by a quite different world from the one their forefathers faced.

First of all, the class nature of the enemy was not the same. In addition they found themselves up against the invading armies of Japanese imperialism, and a little later a fresh threat of invasion from Chiang Kai-shek's American backers, who launched the Korean War and carried their aggression up to the Yalu River.

On top of this, the Chinese peasants established their government in the age of nuclear power, television, jet engines, intercontinental missiles, space rocketry. It was a world dominated by two superpowers, the United States and the Soviet Union—the one tied in with Chiang Kai-shek and standing behind the armies of President Truman and General MacArthur, the other associated with the common struggle against Japan, economic planning, and the immense achievements since 1917 that had lifted Russia out of abysmal backwardness.

Thus the consequence of the victory could not be a mere repetition of China's ancient cycle of revolution and counter-revolution, hinging on the status of agriculture and the private property relations associated with it.

The victory won by the Chinese peasant armies was bound to be shaped by the international context in which it occurred.

Role of armed struggle

The capacity displayed by the Chinese peasants to mobilize themselves in the absence of leadership from the Chinese proletariat gave the armed struggle in China extraordinary force and staying power. Here, too, a special study might provide our movement with very valuable new material.

In checking back in the documents written when China first came up for intensive discussion in our movement, I was struck by the absence of consideration of the role played by the sustained armed struggle.

For instance, in the May 1952 resolution of the International Executive Committee of the Fourth International, which was published in the July–

August 1952 issue of *Fourth International*, there is a list of the ways in which the Soviet bureaucracy sought to block the Chinese Revolution from developing into a proletarian revolution. Among the ways, we are told, was the following: "By the pressure exerted upon the Chinese CP to maintain the tactic of guerrilla warfare, and not to attack the big cities."

This could be taken to mean that Stalin favored rural guerrilla warfare for a prolonged period, but was against urban guerrilla war or, more likely, was against the deployment of the peasant armies to take the big cities when that stage of the guerrilla struggle was reached. At one time, of course, he inspired an opposite course—of attacking cities prematurely.

The resolution contains nothing more than this about the import of the armed struggle in the Chinese Revolution.

It is obvious, I think, that if the 1952 resolution had been written in the light of the Cuban experience, or even in the light of the Algerian experience, that a quite different approach would have been taken on this question.

The truth of it is that quite large forces were involved in the armed struggle even in the early stages. In his successive campaigns to liquidate the so-called soviets set up by Mao in Kiang-si in the early thirties, Chiang Kai-shek utilized armies numbering in the hundreds of thousands.

Three of these massive campaigns were defeated by the revolutionary peasant armies, and in 1931 Mao proclaimed a "Chinese Soviet Republic" in this region. It took two more huge campaigns to dislodge this government and compel Mao to begin the Long March in 1934.

A new base was established in Shensi. For a time the armed struggle against the Chiang Kai-shek government was given up in favor of an alliance with the Chinese bourgeoisie and its political representatives. However, the armed struggle continued for a number of years against the Japanese imperialist forces; and in this struggle the revolutionary peasant armies gained in experience and above all in size until they numbered in the millions. We can well appreciate the pressure they exerted to carry the struggle through to the end.

These armies were highly organized—as was required to defeat the enemy—and thus gave rise to a structure of command with vast ramifications. It would be a great contribution to our knowledge if we could know the absolute size of this network, its relations with other mass organizations, and what changes may have occurred in its outlook after the victory.

Workers and peasants government

The role of the peasant guerrillas and the peasant armies is intimately linked to the role played by the successive governments that were set up in the bases controlled by them.

According to Mao, the government of the Chinese Soviet Republic in Kiangsi had 9,000,000 persons under its rule. In relation to China as a whole that was only a modest number. Just the same it was greater than the population of Cuba today.

In 1937, Mao reduced the "Chinese Soviet Republic" to a "regional authority" covering Shensi, Kansu and Ninghsia. The number of subjects was probably a couple of million at most—say a population something like that in Albania today. Nevertheless from this base, Mao's regional government expanded on a big scale during the war against the Japanese imperialist invaders. Similar regional governments were set up until a hundred million persons or so came under the rule of "Red" or "People's" China.

Thus when the workers and peasants government was established in Peking in 1949, long years of experience in wielding government power had already been accumulated by the apparatus under Mao's command.

How to handle a huge military structure, undertake public works, collect taxes, apply oppressive measures, grant concessions, judge which political currents should be ruthlessly stamped out (such as the Trotskyists) and which should be brought into a "coalition" (such as the "democratic-minded" capitalists and their political parties); how to conduct a foreign policy in keeping with the interests of the apparatus—in short, the whole business of running governmental affairs was already old stuff for the Maoist team.

Thus the workers and peasants government headed by Mao that was established in 1949 had a long background of experience that was invaluable in the task of getting things going and rehabilitating the country after the destruction, dislocations, and havoc China had suffered under Chiang Kai-shek and the imperialist armies of Japan.

In the early years not much attention was paid to the sector of China governed by Mao. Thus it is difficult to form an accurate picture of the way Mao ruled in the period before moving to Peking in 1949 and establishing his fourth capital there. (Juichin, Pao An, Yenan, Peking.)

What kind of justice prevailed under Mao during these decisive years? Was it balanced and fair? Was democracy practiced? Did even a semblance of democracy exist? Or did Mao follow the practices he admired so much in Stalin?

I think that we can make a fairly good guess.

When the peasant armies finally took the cities, they not only put Chiang Kai-shek and his forces to flight, they suppressed every move of the proletariat to engage as an independent force in the revolutionary upsurge. In following this policy, Mao was not initiating something new, he was continuing what he had practiced for years. Stalinism was congenial in the new regime.

Stalinism, a temporary phenomenon

Perhaps this is the place to consider Trotsky's thesis that Stalinism was a temporary phenomenon, doomed to disappear with the advance of the revolution. This is absolutely correct on a historic scale. Trotsky based it on the consideration that with the success of the proletarian revolution in one or more advanced capitalist countries, the standard of living could be raised so rapidly as to destroy Stalinism economically, since Stalinism arose as a product of a backward economy in a country subjected to extreme isolation and pressure by world capitalism.

But Trotsky did not speculate on what might occur if the proletarian revolution in the advanced capitalist countries was delayed for several more decades while the revolution conquered in areas still more backward than Czarist Russia.

We have seen what happens in this case. It is a matter of history. Stalinism is temporarily strengthened and its death agony is prolonged.

Trotsky's thesis nevertheless caused many comrades to scan Maoism with the hope that it might prove to be anti-Stalinist and thus provide early confirmation of Trotsky's prognosis on the historic fate of Stalinism.

Mao's policy in Indonesia and his course in the "cultural revolution" have shown how misplaced these hopes were.

Birth of Chinese workers state

Let us continue with our analysis.

The workers and peasants government that began wielding power in Peking in 1949 was decisive in another respect in shaping the ultimate outcome of the Chinese Revolution.

It was this government that finally destroyed the capitalist state and established a workers state in China. This took place despite Mao's "New Democracy" program of maintaining capitalism for a prolonged period. The tasks faced by the new regime, particularly when they were compounded by the aggression of American imperialism in Korea, were of such order that they could be met only through economic forms that are socialist in principle.

The establishment of a workers state in China offered the most striking testimony as to the validity of the basic premise in Trotsky's theory of the permanent revolution; namely, the tendency of revolutions in the backward countries to transcend the bourgeois-democratic phase and turn into socialist revolutions. Our movement has correctly placed a great deal of stress on this; it is not necessary for me to repeat it here.

What I should like to call special attention to is the link in the revolutionary process through which this qualitative leap was made possible—the workers and peasants government.

From the theoretical point of view this is the item of greatest interest, for it was this government that set up the economic forms modeled on those existing in the Soviet Union, repeating what had happened in Eastern Europe and Yugoslavia.

The possibility of workers and peasants governments coming to power had been visualized by the Communist International at the Fourth Congress in 1922. But the Bolsheviks held that such governments, set up by petty-bourgeois parties could not be characterized as proletarian dictatorships, that is, workers states.

The Bolsheviks were firmly convinced that petty-bourgeois parties, even though they went so far as to establish a workers and peasants government, could never move forward to establish a workers state. Only a revolutionary Communist party, rooted in the working class on a mass scale so as to be able to lead it into action, could do that.

The experience in China showed that in at least one case history had decreed otherwise.

This came on top of the experience in Yugoslavia and in Eastern Europe where it can be argued that the implications were not so clear cut because of the role played by the Soviet armies, the catastrophe suffered by German imperialism, and the revolutionary crisis suffered by the other capitalist powers in Europe.

It was precisely because of the adjustment that would be required in the hypothesis advanced by the Fourth Congress of the Communist International that our party moved so cautiously and sought to explore every possible alternative before it agreed to recognize that a workers state had been established in China. We take a very serious attitude toward theory.

The thoroughness with which we sought to examine the consequences of the Chinese experience served as good preparation for what happened in Cuba some ten years after the Chinese victory. We were able to follow the pattern of events in Cuba with ease.

The most gratifying aspect of this from the standpoint of theory was that the pattern of the Cuban Revolution decisively confirmed the principal conclusions we had reached with regard to China.

Cuba and Algeria

The key item in Cuba was the workers and peasants government established in 1959 by a petty-bourgeois political force, the July 26 Movement.

As in the case of China, this new Cuban government, which had been brought to power through a hard-fought armed struggle and a revolution of the most deep-going and popular character, could not meet the giant tasks it faced, particularly in face of the violent reaction of U.S. imperialism, without toppling the capitalist structure and establishing economic forms that were socialist in principle.

Once again, these were modeled by and large on those in the Soviet Union. Even more than in the case of China, the very possibility of a workers state in Cuba of any durability hinged on the existence of the Soviet Union. The appearance of a viable workers state in Cuba was thus a consequence, in the final analysis, of the victory of the Soviet Union in World War II.

The pattern was similarly visible in the Algerian Revolution. In this instance, however, no workers state was established. Instead the workers and peasants government was brought down by a military coup d'état in June 1965 after some three years in power.

This was proof that the establishment of a workers and peasants government does not automatically guarantee the subsequent establishment of a workers state.

In the case of Cuba, a significant new development was to be observed. The leadership that came to power, while it was petty-bourgeois, was not trained in the school of Stalinism. It stood to the left of the Cuban Communist Party.

The importance of this cannot be overemphasized. The team headed by Fidel Castro and Che Guevara constituted the first contingent of a new generation of revolutionists that cannot be brainwashed by either Moscow or Peking.

Trend toward classic norm

On the broad scale of the post World War II period, this constitutes a watershed.

The deformation of the revolutionary process in Eastern Europe, in Yugoslavia, in China, in North Korea and North Vietnam was a resultant of the revolutionary upsurge following World War II coupled with the temporary strengthening of Stalinism.

The expansion of Stalinism, however, intensified its internal contradictions and this led to a series of crises that finally culminated in the Sino-Soviet conflict and the spread of "polycentrism." Stalinism has thus been greatly weakened. Even in its Maoist form, Stalinism now faces an increasingly dim future.

On the other hand, the establishment of a series of workers states as the consequence of successful revolutions has greatly strengthened the world revolution and its perspectives.

This means a growing tendency internationally toward a revolutionary pattern that comes much closer to the classic norm in which the proletariat moves into the foreground. Evidence of this is to be seen in the shifting of the axis of revolutionary struggles in the backward countries from the countryside to the cities. The events in France in May–June 1968 showed what explosive potential now exists in the imperialist centers of the West. The ghetto uprisings in the United States and the upsurge among the student youth internationally have offered further corroboration of the trend.

We can conclude from this that the next revolutionary victory, wherever it comes, will in all likelihood go even further than the Cuban Revolution in departing from the deformation imposed by the pernicious heritage of Stalinism. The Leninist norm, calling for construction of a fully conscious revolutionary-socialist combat party, will acquire full force and validity as revolutionary situations develop in the strongholds of world capitalism.

Consequences

What are the main consequences of viewing the Chinese Revolution along the lines I have indicated so far as the current discussion is concerned?

First of all, I would say that it is much easier to see the role played by the peasantry and its petty-bourgeois leadership. We can call them what they are, *petty-bourgeois*, without seeking to conjure away this fact or to ameliorate it by speculating that after all these forces must have been proletarian in some shape or fashion, otherwise the peasantry and the Stalinized Communist Party could not have played the role they did.

Secondly, we can see much more easily how a proletarian element did finally come into play in the Chinese Revolution through the governmental power that established economic forms modeled on those of the Soviet Union.

Thirdly, we can more easily see the continuous thread of Stalinism in China from the very beginning up to the current stage marked by the crisis and fierce factional struggle of the "cultural revolution." It is not necessary to look for periods in which Stalinism presumably vanished—only to reappear. We eliminate this awkward hypothesis which would require us to explain how Stalinism in China could have died in the flames of a peasant upheaval only to arise again from the ashes of the "great proletarian cultural revolution."

Fourthly, we can much more easily grasp the origins of the bureaucracy in China, how it was shaped by Stalinism as it came into being, and what a substantial element this bureaucracy actually is in the Chinese social and political scene.

Fifthly, we are in better position to understand the interrelationship between Mao's domestic and foreign policies, and particularly in the case of his foreign policy to see how its basic design is to safeguard and advance the position of the bureaucratic ruling caste and why this gives his foreign policy its nationalistic "peaceful coexistence" characteristics and its capacity to alternate between rank opportunism and adventuristic ultraleftism. It becomes easier to see the true origin of Mao's foreign policy and to avoid the error of mistaking the *resultant* of the clash between Peking's policy and the contending policies of other countries with what Mao seeks to achieve.

Sixthly, by considering the pattern of the Chinese Revolution in conjunction with the patterns in Eastern Europe, Yugoslavia, Cuba, Algeria, we can much more readily appreciate the limitations of the lessons to be drawn. It is easier to avoid unwarranted and incorrect extrapolations that could prove very misleading and dangerous.

In mentioning these consequences, I should like to stress that they are derivative. They follow from viewing the Chinese Revolution in the way I have suggested.

What is most important, of course, is to weigh the validity of this analysis of the pattern of the Chinese Revolution and its connection with the patterns in Eastern Europe, Yugoslavia, Cuba, and Algeria.

In any case, as the discussion develops internationally on this subject, the most fruitful contributions may well be those that seek to fill in the extensive gaps that still exist in our knowledge of some of the phases of the Chinese Revolution that are of the greatest interest from the standpoint of theory.

State capitalism

Postscript:

Because of time limitations it was not possible for me to do more at the convention than barely refer during my summary to a point that should be considered logically in conjunction with the question of the degenerated or deformed workers states and their relationship to Stalinism. This is the peculiar state structures of countries like Egypt and Burma.

As is well known, in these countries the government has taken over the bulk of the means of production with the exception of agriculture.

The nationalizations are so extensive, in fact, that quantitatively the situation appears comparable to what exists in the workers states. As a result it is tempting to equate them with workers states; and this has been done—incorrectly so—by various currents.

One procedure of those who make this error is to call them workers states. Another is to call them state capitalist; but—still equating them with workers states—to call countries like the Soviet Union and China "state capitalist."

The essential difference between states like Egypt and genuine workers states is to be found in their different origin. In every instance, the workers states, whether deformed or otherwise, have emerged as products of revolutions. Through armed struggle, through upheavals involving the masses on an immense scale, the people have overthrown their capitalist oppressors, displacing them from power in the most thoroughgoing way.

In countries like Egypt, upheavals on this scale have not occurred. The usual pattern is that a sector of the officer caste takes over, generally through a coup d'état, occasionally ratified through partial mobilization of the masses, who, of course, are in favor of ousting the old regime.

The new government is fearful of the masses. One of the first things it does is to block the masses from mobilizing, at least in a massive revolutionary way. The new government aims at giving capitalism a new lease on life after a period in incubation under auspices of the state apparatus.

The officialdom is thoroughly aware of the ultimate perspective, and conducts itself accordingly. How the state machinery is used to spawn millionaires was graphically demonstrated in Mexico.

It is obvious that the qualitative nature of nationalizations is determined by whether they originate in a thoroughgoing revolutionary struggle or in measures undertaken by a sector of the officer caste or their political representatives, who may even have in mind forestalling a popular revolution by setting up a simulacrum of a workers state. This phenomenon can be quite correctly placed under the general heading of state capitalism.

What is demonstrated by the extensive nationalizations in countries like Egypt—and the less extensive ones in Mexico and elsewhere in Latin America—is the enormous pressure being exerted on a world scale to bring capitalism to a close and to move into the epoch of socialism. Private capitalism has become so antiquated, so outdated, that capitalist governments everywhere are compelled to intervene more and more extensively in the very management of industry if they hope to prolong the death agony of the system a bit longer.

The growth of state capitalism also testifies to the depth of the crisis in revolutionary leadership observable on an international scale. Prime responsibility for this lies with Stalinism.

The overhead cost of the many betrayals of the most promising revolutionary openings, from Germany in the early thirties to Indonesia three decades later, can be measured, among other ways, by the growth of statism, the direct intervention of the capitalist state in the economic system.

The importance of the occurrence of a *revolution*, as one of the criteria in determining that a workers state has come into existence is very clear in the case of Cuba.

Because they do not recognize this criterion, the Healyites refuse to acknowledge that a workers state exists in Cuba. They lump Cuba with Egypt, Burma, Syria, and so on.

They are inconsistent in not placing China and Yugoslavia in the same category. They seek to avoid this inconsistency by making the existence of *Stalinism* the decisive criterion. This shows that in the final analysis they are incapable of distinguishing between revolution and counterrevolution.

The qualitative difference that a revolution makes in nationalizations is evident in the difference in durability of the takeovers in countries where a revolution has occurred and countries where it has not occurred.

This is because of the fact that the old ruling class is smashed in the one instance and only temporarily displaced in the other while the state structure is used to rejuvenate the system. The marked difference in popular consciousness is likewise of prime importance.

Cuba and Burma offer striking examples of these differences.

A comparative study along these lines would undoubtedly prove highly instructive.

COMMUNIST CONTINUITY AND PROGRAM

New!
Revolution and the Road to Peace in Colombia
The Example of the Cuban Revolution
FIDEL CASTRO

"No crime can be committed in the name of revolution," Fidel Castro declares, drawing from the example set by working people of Cuba as they took state power out of the hands of its capitalist rulers. In 2008, as part of efforts to end six decades of armed conflict in Colombia, he shared the exemplary record of Cuba's revolutionary struggle with the Revolutionary Armed Forces of Colombia (FARC) and the world. $10. Also in Spanish.

New Expanded Edition!
Cosmetics, Fashion, and the Exploitation of Women
MARY-ALICE WATERS
JOSEPH HANSEN, EVELYN REED

"Norms of beauty and fashion are inseparable from the class struggle." That's the title of the opening chapter of this timely new edition of a lively 1950s debate in the *Militant*, a socialist newsweekly. How cosmetics and fashion monopolies rake in profits from social insecurities of women and adolescents. Why women's integration into the workforce and unions is a major advance in the fight for emancipation. A Marxist classic on the origins of women's oppression and the working-class road forward. $15. Also in Spanish, French, Farsi, Greek.

Lenin's Final Fight
Speeches and Writings, 1922–23
V.I. LENIN

In 1922 and 1923, V.I. Lenin, central leader of the world's first socialist revolution, waged what was to be his last political battle—one that was lost after his death. At stake was whether that revolution, and the international communist movement it led, would remain on the revolutionary proletarian course that brought workers and peasants to power in Russia in 1917. $17. Also in Spanish, Farsi, Greek.

Revolutionary Continuity
Marxist Leadership in the U.S.
The Early Years, 1848–1917
Birth of the Communist Movement, 1918–1922
FARRELL DOBBS

"Successive generations of proletarian revolutionists have participated in the movements of the working class and its allies. . . . Marxists today owe them not only homage for their deeds. We also have a duty to learn what they did wrong as well as right so their errors are not repeated." —*Farrell Dobbs*. Two volumes, $17 each.

The Transitional Program for Socialist Revolution
LEON TROTSKY

The Socialist Workers Party program, drafted by Bolshevik leader Trotsky in 1938, still guides communists the world over. The party "uncompromisingly gives battle to all political groupings tied to the apron strings of the bourgeoisie. Its task—the abolition of capitalism's domination. Its aim—socialism. Its method—the proletarian revolution." $17. Also in Farsi.

The Struggle for a Proletarian Party
JAMES P. CANNON

"The workers of America have power enough to topple the structure of capitalism at home and to lift the whole world with them when they rise," Cannon asserts. On the eve of World War II, a founder of the communist movement in the US and leader of the Communist International in Lenin's time defends the program and party-building norms of Bolshevism. $20. Also in Spanish and Farsi.

CAPITALIST CRISIS AND THE FIGHT FOR WORKERS POWER

The Jewish Question
A Marxist Interpretation
ABRAM LEON

The battle against reactionary forces aiming to exterminate the Jews remains central to world politics, as shown by the genocidal October 2023 pogrom in Israel. Why is Jew-hatred still raising its ugly head? What are its class roots? Why, as Abram Leon explains, is there no solution "independent of the world proletarian revolution"? Revised translation, new introduction, 40 pages of illustrations and maps. $17. Also in Spanish, French, Greek.

Cuba and the Coming American Revolution
JACK BARNES

This is a book about the example set by the Cuban people that socialist revolution is not only necessary—it can be made. A book about the struggles of workers and other exploited producers in the imperialist heartland, and the youth attracted to them. About the class struggle in the US, where the revolutionary capacities of working people are as utterly discounted by the ruling powers as were those of the Cuban toilers. $10. Also in Spanish, French, Farsi.

Opening Guns of World War III: Washington's Assault on Iraq
JACK BARNES

The murderous assault on Iraq in 1990–91 heralded increasingly sharp conflicts among imperialist powers, growing instability of capitalism, and more wars. Also includes:

1945: When US Troops Said 'No!' by Mary-Alice Waters

Lessons from the Iran-Iraq War by Samad Sharif

In *New International* no. 7. $14. Also in Spanish, French, Farsi.

Teamster Rebellion
FARRELL DOBBS

The 1934 strikes that won union recognition for truckers and warehouse workers in Minneapolis and helped pave the way for the working-class social movement that built the industrial unions. The first of four volumes by a central leader of these battles and of the Socialist Workers Party. $16. Also in Spanish, French, Farsi, Greek.

Capitalism's Long Hot Winter Has Begun
JACK BARNES

Today's global capitalist crisis is but the opening stage of decades of economic, financial, and social convulsions and class battles. Class-conscious workers confront this historic turning point for imperialism with confidence, Jack Barnes writes, drawing satisfaction from being "in their face" as we chart a revolutionary course to take power. In *New International* no. 12. $14. Also in Spanish, French, Farsi, Arabic, Greek.

The Third International After Lenin
LEON TROTSKY

Leon Trotsky's 1928 defense of the Marxist course that had guided the Communist International in its early years. Writing in the heat of political battle, Trotsky addresses the key challenge facing working people today: building communist parties throughout the world capable of leading workers and farmers to take power. $20. Also in Farsi.

The Clintons' Anti-Working-Class Record
Why Washington Fears Working People
JACK BARNES

What working people need to know about the profit-driven course of Democrats and Republicans alike over the last three decades. And the political awakening of workers seeking to understand and resist the capitalist rulers' assaults. $10. Also in Spanish, French, Farsi, Greek.